The Spiritual Guide which Disentangles the Soul

MIGUEL DE MOLINOS

GodSounds
"Where Faith is Heard"

More books available:

Heavenly Authority: The Right of the Believer by John G Lake

Divine Healing by John G Lake

Spiritual Gifts: What God Gives to Us by Smith Wigglesworth

The Faith Collection: Three Books in One by Smith Wigglesworth

Intimacy with Jesus by Madame Guyon

Words from the Almighty by William S. Crockett Jr.

Polycarp's Letter to the Philipians & His Martyrdom by St. Polycarp

Finney Gold: Words that Helped Birth Revival by Charles Finney

Walking with God by George Whitefield

Looking to publish your own book? Or need your book made into an audiobook?
Go to GodSounds.com

DEDICATION

The reprinting of this book is dedicated to my brother Daniel
Mironichenko. Thank you for being an amazing friend!
Jori

CONTENTS

ACKNOWLEDGMENTS

And the LORD shall guide thee continually, and satisfy thy soul in drought, and make fat thy bones: and thou shalt be like a watered garden, and like a spring of water, whose waters fail not. Isaiah 58:11

The Author to the Reader

THERE IS NOTHING MORE DIFFICULT, than to please all People, not more easie and common than to censure Books that come abroad in the World. All Books, without exception, that see the light, run the common Risk of both these inconveniences, though they may be sheltered under the most sublime Protection, what will become of this little Book then, which hath no Patronage? The Subject whereof being mystical, and not well-seasoned; carries along with it the common censure, and will seem insipid? Kind Reader, if you understand it not, be not therefore apt to censure the same.

The Natural Man may hear and read these Spiritual Matters, but he can never comprehend them, as St. Paul saith; (I Cor.c.2) The Natural Man receiveth not the things of the Spirit of God. If you condemn it, you condemn your self to the number of the wise men of this World, of who St. Denis says, that God imparts not this Wisdom to them, as he does to the simple and humble, though in the opinion of Men they be ignorant.

Mystical knowledge proceeds not from Wit, but from Experience; it is not invented, but proved; not read, but received; and is therefore most secure and efficacious, of great help and plentiful in fruit; it enters not (Mat.II.) into the Soul by Ears, nor by the continual Reading of Books, but by the free Infusion of the Holy Ghost, whose Grace with most delightful intimacy, is communicated to the simple and lowly.

There are some Learned Men, who have never read these Matters, and some Spiritual Men that hitherto have hardly relished them and therefore both condemn them, the one out of Ignorance, and the other for want of Experience.

Besides, it is certain, that he who hath not the experience of this sweetness, cannot pass a Judgement upon these Mysterious Secrets; nay, rather he'll be Scandalized (as many are) when he hears of the Wonders which the Divine Love is wont to work in Souls, because he finds no such

1

Rarities in his own. Who shall limit the goodness of God, whose Arm is not shortened, but that he can do now what he hath wrought at other times? God calls neither the strongest nor the richest for their Merit; but calls rather the weakest and most wretched, that his infinite mercy may shine forth the more.

This Science is not Theoretical, but Practical, wherein Experience surpasses the most refined and ingenious Speculation. Hence it was that St. Tiresia admonished her Ghostly Father, that he should not confer about Spiritual Matters, but with Spiritual Men; Because, said she, if they know but one way, or if they have stopped mid-way, there is no success to be expected.

It will soon appear that he hath no experience of this practical and mystical Science, who shall condemn the Doctrine of this Book, and who hath not read St. Dennis, St. Austin, St. Gregory, St. Bernard, St. Thomas, St. Bonaventure, and many other Saints and Doctors approved by the Church, who like expert men, approve, commend, and teach the Practice of this Doctrine.

It is to be taken notice of, that the Doctrine of this Book instructs not all sorts of Persons, but those only who have the Senses and Passions well mortified, who have already advanced and made progress in Prayer, and are called by God to the inward way, who encourages and guides them, freeing them from the obstacles which hinder the course to perfect Contemplation.

I have taken care to have the Style of this Book devote, chaste, and useful, without the ornament of polite Sentences, ostentation of Eloquence, or Theological Niceties, my only scope was to teach the Naked Truth, with humility, sincerity and perspicuity.

It is not to be wondered at that new Spiritual Books are every day published in the World, because God hath always new Light to communicate, and Souls stand always in need of these Instructions. All things have not been said, nor every thing written, hence it is that there will be Writing to the end of the World. Wonderful were the Lights that God Almighty communicated to his Church by means of the Angelical Doctor St. Thomas, and at the hour of his Death, he himself said that the Divine Majesty had at that instant communicated to him so much light, that all he had before written came short of it. God has, then, and always will have new Lights to communicate, without any diminution to his own Infinite Wisdom.

The many and grievous pains and difficulties of the inward way ought not to make a Soul despond, because it is but reasonable that a thing of great value should cost dear. Be of good comfort, and believe, that not only those which are here represented, but many others also will be overcome with the Grace of God and internal Fortitude.

It was never my design to treat of Contemplation, nor in defence of it, as many have done who have learnedly and speculatively published whole Books, full of efficacious Reasons, Doctrines and Authorities of Saints and of the Holy Scripture, for confuting the Opinion of those who without any ground have condemned, and do condemn it.

The Experience of many Years (by reason of the many Souls who have trusted to my insufficiency, for their conduct in the inward way, to which they have been called) hath convinced me of the great necessity they are in of having the obstacles taken out of their way, the inclinations, affections and allurements removed, which wholly hinder the course and obstruct the way to perfect Contemplation.

This whole Practical Book tends chiefly to this end, because it is not enough to ascertain the inward way of Contemplation, if the obstacles be not taken out of the way of those Souls that are called and assured, which hinder their progress and spiritual flight; For which end I have made use rather of what God out of his infinite mercy hath inspired into me, and taught me, than of any thing that the speculative reading of Books has suggested unto me, or furnished me with.

Sometimes (though very seldom) I quote the Authority of some practical and experienc'd Author, to show that the Doctrine which is here taught is not singular and rare. It hath been my first scope then, not to ascertain the inward way but to disentangle and unpester it; My next hath been to instruct the Spiritual Divertors, that they may not stop those Souls in their course which are called by these secret Paths to internal Peace and Supreme Felicity. God of his infinite Mercy grant, that an end so much desired may be obtained.

I hope in God, that some of those Souls, whom his Divine Majesty calls to this knowledg, will find profit from what I have writ; for whose sake I shall reckon my pains very well employed. This has been the only But of my desire, and if God (as certainly he will) accept and approve those pure desires, I shall be content and have my reward.

Farewell

Preface

First Advertisement

By two ways one may go to God, the first by Meditation and Discourse or Reasoning; the second by pure Faith and Contemplation.

1. There are two ways of going to God, the one by Consideration and Mental Discourse, and the other by the Purity of Faith, an indistinct, general and confused knowledge. The first is called Meditation, the second Internal Recollection, or acquir'd Contemplation. The first is of Beginners, the second of Proficients. The first is sensible and material, the second more naked, pure and internal.

2. When the Soul is already accustomed to discourse of Mysteries, by the help of imagination, and the use of corporal Images; being carried from Creature to Creature, and from Knowledg to Knowledg (though with very little of that which it wants) and from these to the Creator; Then God is wont to take that Soul by the hand (if rather he calls it not in the very beginning, and leads it without ratiocination by the way of pure Faith) making the Intellect pass by all considerations and reasonings, draws it forward, and raises it out of this material and sensible state, making it under a simple and obscure knowledge of Faith, wholly aspire to its Bridegroom upon the wings of Love, without any farther necessity of the perswasions and informations of the Intellect, to make it love him, because in that manner the Soul's love would be very scanty, much dependent on Creature, stinted to drops, and these too but falling with pauses and intervals.

3. By how much less it depends on Creatures, and the more it relies on God alone, and his secret documents, by the mediation of pure Faith, the more durable, firm, and strong will that Love be. After the Soul hath

already acquired the knowledg which all the meditations and corporal Images of Creatures can give her; it, now, the Lord raise her out of that state, by stripping her of ratiocination, and leaving her in divine darkness, to the end she may march in the streight Way, and by pure Faith, let her be guided, and not love with the scantiness and tenuity that these direct; but let her suppose that the whole World, and all that the most refined conceptions of the wisest understandings can tell her, are nothing, and that the goodness and beauty of her beloved, infinitely surpasses all their knowledg, being perswaded that all Creatures are too rude to inform her, and to conduct her to the true knowledg of God.

4. She ought then to advance forward with her love, leaving all her understanding behind. Let her love God as he is in himself, and not as her imagination says he is, and frames him to her; And if she cannot know him as he is in himself, let her love him without knowing him under the obscure veils of Faith; in the same manner as a Son who hath never seen his Father, but fully believing those who have given him information of him, loves him, as if he had already seen him.

5. The Soul, from which Mental Discourse is taken, ought not to strain her self, nor solicitously seek for more clear and particular knowledge, but even without the supports of sensible consolations or notices, with poverty of spirit, and deprived of all that the natural appetite requires; continue quiet, firm and constant, letting the Lord work his work, though she may seem to be alone, exhausted and full of darkness: and though this appear to her to be idleness, it is only of her own sensible and material activity, not of God's, who is working true knowledg in her.

6. Finally, the more the Spirit ascends, the more it is taken off of sensible Objects. Many are the Souls who have arrived and do arrive at this gate, but few have passed or do pass it, for want of the experimental guide, and those who have had, and actually have it, for want of a true subjection and intire submission.

7. They'll say, that the Will will not love; but be unactive, if the Intellect understand not clearly and distinctly, it being a received Maxim, that that which is not known, cannot be loved. To this it is answered, that tho' the Intellect understand not distinctly by ratiocination, Images and Considerations, yet it understands and knows by an obscure, general and confused Faith; which knowledg, tho' so obscure, indistinct, and general, and being supernatural, hath nevertheless a more clear and perfect cognition of God, than any sensible and particular notice, that can be formed in this life, because all corporal and sensible representation is infinitely distant from God.

8. We know God more perfectly (says St. Denis - *Mystic. Theol. c.I.§.2*) by Negatives, than by Affirmatives. We think more highly of God, by knowing that he is incomprehensible, and above all our capacity, than by conceiving

him under any image or created beauty, according to our rude understanding. A greater esteem and love then will flow from this confused, obscure and negative, than from any other sensible and distinct way; because that is more proper to God, and abstracted from creatures; and this, on the contrary, the more it depends on creatures, the less it hath of God.

Second Advertisement

Declaring what Meditation and Contemplation are, and the difference that is betwixt them.

9. St. John Damascene (*Lib. 3. de fide, c.24.*) and other Saints say, that Prayer is a sallying out or elevation of the Mind to God. God is above all creatures, and the Soul cannot see him, nor converse with him, if it raise not it self above them all. This friendly conversation, which the Soul hath with God, that's to say, in Prayer, is divided into Meditation and Contemplation.

10. When the Mind considers the Mysteries of our holy Faith with attention, to know the truth of them, reasoning upon the particulars, and weighing the circumstances of the same, for the exciting of affections in the Will; this mental discourse and pious Act is properly called Meditation.

11. When the Soul already knows the truth (either by a habit acquired through reasoning, or because the Lord hath given it particular light) and fixes the eyes of the Mind on the demonstrated truth, beholding it sincerely with quietness and silence, without any necessity of considerations, ratiocinations, or other proofs of conviction, and the will loves it, admiring and delighting it self therein; This properly is called the Prayer of Faith, the Prayer of Rest, Internal Recognition or Contemplation.

Which St. Thomas (*2.2.q.180. Art. 3. p.4*) with all the mystical Masters says, *is a sincere, sweet, and still view of the eternal truth without ratiocination, or reflexion.* But if the Soul rejoyces in, or eyes the effects of God in the creatures, and amongst them, in the humanity of our Lord Christ, as the most perfect of all, this is not perfect Contemplation, as St. Thomas (ibidem.) affirms, since all these are means for knowing of God as he is in himself: And although the humanity of Christ be the most holy and perfect means for going to God, the chief instrument of our salvation, and the channel through which we receive all the good we hope for, nevertheless the humanity is not the chief good, which consists in seeing God; but as Jesus Christ is more by his divinity than his humanity, so he that thinks and fixes his contemplation always on God (because the divinity is united to the humanity) always thinks on, and beholds Jesus Christ, especially, the contemplative man, in whom Faith is more sincere, pure and exercised.

13. As often as the end is obtained, the means cease, and when the Ship arrives in the Harbour the voyage is over. So if the Soul after it hath been toiled and carried by means of meditation, arrives at the stillness, tranquility, and rest of Contemplation, it ought then to cut off all reasonings, and rest quiet with an amorous attention, and simple Vision of God; seeing and loving him, sweetly rejecting all the imaginations that present themselves, calming the Mind in that Divine Presence, recollecting the Memory, and fixing it wholly on God, being contented with a general and confused knowledge, which is had by the Mediation of Faith, applying the whole Will to love him, wherein consists all their fruit of enjoyment.

14. St. Denis (*Myst. Theol.*) says, *As for you, most dear Timothy, in applying your self to Mystical Speculations, abstract from the Senses and Operations of the Intellect; from all sensible and intelligible Objects, and Universally from all things that are, and are not; and in an unknown and inexpressible Way, as much as lies in the power of Man, raise your self to the Union of him, who is above all Nature and Knowledge.* Thus far the Saint.

15. It concerns us then, to forsake all created, sensible, intelligible and affected Beings; and in short, every thing that is, and is not, that we may cast our selves into the loving Bosom of God, who will restore to us as much as we have left, increasing in us strength and power to love him more ardently, whose love will maintain it self within this Holy and Blessed Silence, which is of more worth than all Acts joined together

16. St. Thomas (*Quest. 27. 2.ad secuedum ar.*) says, *It is the least thing, that the Understanding can know of God in this Life, but much what the Will can have of Love.*

17. When the Soul attains to this state, it ought wholly to retreat within it self, in its own pure and profound Center; where the Image of God is, there is amorous attention, silence, the forgetfulness of all things, the application of the Will, with perfect resignation, hearing and talking with God hand to hand, and in such manner, as if there was no other but them two in the World.

18. Good reason have the Saints to say, that Meditation operates with toyl, and with fruit; Contemplation without toyl, with quiet, rest, peace, delight, and far greater fruit. Meditation sows, and Contemplation reaps; Meditation seeks, and Contemplation finds; Meditation chews the Food, Contemplation tasts and feeds on it.

19. All this was said by Mystical Bernard, upon these Words of our Savior; *Querite & invenietis; pulsate & aperietur vobis. Lectio opponit ori solidum cibum, Meditatio frangit; Oratio japorem conciliat, Contemplatio est ipsa dulcedo que jucundat & resicit.* Thus ye have an account what Meditation and Contemplation are, and the difference that occurs betwixt them.

Third Advertisement

What is the Difference betwixt the Acquired and Active Contemplation, and the Infused and Passive. With the Signs whereby it is known, when God will have the Soul to pass from Meditation, to Contemplation.

20. There are moreover two ways of Contemplation: The one is Imperfect, Active and Acquired; The other Infused and Passive. The Active (whereof we have treated hitherto) is that which may be attained to by our Diligence, assisted with Divine Grace; we gathering together the Faculties and Senses, and preparing our selves by every way that God would have. So says *Boias* and *Arnaia.*

21. St. Bernard (Psal. 85) recommends this Active Contemplation, discoursing upon these Words, *Audiam quid loquatur in me Deus.* And he says *Optimam partem elegit Maria, licet non minoris (fortasse) meriti sit apud Deum humilis conversatio Marthæ, sed de electione Maria laudatur: quoniam illa omnino (quo ad nos spectat) eligenda, hæc vero si injungitur patienter est toleranda.*

22. In like manner St. Thomas (*Secund.q.182. art. 2.&3.*) inculcates this acquired contemplation in the following words; *Quanto homo animam suam, vel alterius propinquius deo conjungit, tanto sacrificium est deo magis acceptum, unde magis acceptum est deo quod aliquis animam suam & aliorum applicet contemplationi quam actioni.* Very clear Words to stop the Mouth of those who condemn acquired contemplation.

23. How much the nearer a man approaches his own Soul, or the Soul of another to God, so much the more acceptable is the Sacrifice to God; from whence it is inferred (concludes the same Saint) that the application of a man's own Soul, or the procuring that of anothers to Contemplation, is more acceptable to God, than the applying of the same to Action. It cannot be said, that the Saint speaks here of infused Contemplation, because it is not in the power of man, to apply himself to the infused, but to the acquired.

24. Though it be said, that we may with the Lord's help, set our selves to acquired contemplation; nevertheless, no man ought of his own Head to be so bold, as to pass from the state of Meditation to this, without the counsel of an expert Director, who shall clearly know whether his Soul be called by God to this inward way; or for want of a Director, the Soul it self is to know it by some Book, that treats of these Matters, sent to him by Divine Providence, for discovering that, which without knowing what it was, he experimentally felt within his own Heart. But though by means of the light which that Book gives him he may obtain assurance enough, to leave Meditation for the quiet of contemplation, yet his Soul will still retain an ardent desire of being more perfectly instructed.

25. And to the end it may receive good Instruction in order to that point, I'll here give it the Signs whereby it shall know that call to

contemplation. The first and chief is, an inability to meditate, and if the Soul meditate, it will perform it with much disquiet and irksomness, provided that proceed not from the indisposition of Nature, or a melancholy Humour, or a Dryness, springing from the want of Preparation.

26. It will be known not to be any of these defects, but rather a true call, when that Soul passes a Day, a Month; nay, and many Months, without being able to discourse in Prayer. *The Lord guides the Soul by Contemplation* (says the holy Mother Teresa) *and the Mind finds it self much disabled from meditating the Passion of Christ, since Meditation is nothing else but a seeking of God; the Soul once finding him, and retaining the Custom of seeking him of new, by the operation of the Will, it will not be baffled with the Intellect.* Thus far the Saint.

27. The second Sign is, that though it is wanting in sensible Devotion, yet it covets Solitude, and avoids conversation.

The third, that the reading of godly Books is usually tedious to it, because they speak not of the Internal Sweetness that is in its Heart, tho' it know it not.

The fourth, that though it find it self destitute of ratiocination, yet it hath a firm purpose of persevering in Prayer. The fifth is, that it will experience a sense (with great confusion) of it self, abhorring guilt, and entertaining a higher esteem of God.

28. The other *Contemplation* is perfect and infused. *Wherein* (as St. Teresa says) *God speaks to a man, sequestrating his intelect, questioning his thought, and seizing (as they say) the word in his mouth; so that if he would, he cannot speak, but with great pain. He understands, that without the noise of words, the Divine Master is instructing him, suspending all his powers and faculties, because if at that time they should operate, they would do more hurt than good. These rejoyce, but know not how they rejoyce; the Soul is inflamed with love, and conceives not how it loves; it knows that it enjoys what it desires, and knows not the manner of that enjoyment; well it knows, that that is not enjoyment which the intellect longs for. The Will embraces it, without understanding how; but being unable to understand any thing, perceives it is not that good, which can be merited by all the labours put together which are suffered upon earth for gaining it. It is a gift of the Lord of the Soul, and of Heaven, who in the end gives as he is, and to whom he pleases as he pleases: Such is his Majesty in this, that it does every thing, and his operation is above our nature.* All this we have from holy Mother, in her *Way to Perfection,* chap. 25. From whence it follows, that this *Contemplation* is infused, and freely given by the Lord to whom he pleases.

Fourth Advertisement

The Burden of this Book consisting in rooting out the Rebellion of our own Will, that we may attain to internal Peace.

29. The way of inward Peace, is in all things to be conform to the pleasure and disposition of the Divine Will. (*Hugo Cardinalisin Pf. 13.*) *In omnibus debemus subjicere volis tatem nostram voluntatis divine hæc est enim pax voluntati nostra ut sit per omnia confirmis voluntati divine.* Such as would have all things succeed and come to pass according to their own fancy, are not come to know this way, *Viam pacis non cognos verunt*, and therefore lead a harsh and bitter life, always restless and out of humour without treading the way of Peace, which consists in a total conformity to the will of God.

30. This conformity is the sweet yoke that introduces us into the regions of internal Peace and serenity. Hence we may know, that the rebellion of our Will is the chief occasion of our disquiet; and that because we will not submit to the sweet yoke of the Divine Will, we suffer so many streights and perturbations. O Soul! if we submitted our own to the Divine Will, and to all his Disposition, what tranquility should we feel! what sweet peace! what inward serenity! what supreme felicity and earnest of bliss!. This then is to be the burden of this Book: May it please God to give me his Divine Light, for discovering the secret Paths of this Inward Way, and chief Felicity of perfect Peace.

CHAPTER 1

The Spiritual Guide which Leads the Soul to the Fruition of Inward Peace

Of the Darkness, Dryness, and Temptations wherewith God purges Souls, and of Internal Recollection.

SECTION ONE: *To the end God may rest in the Soul, the Heart is always to be kept peaceable in whatsoever Disquiet, Temptation and Tribulation.*

1. Thou art to know, that thy Soul is the Center, Habitation, and the Kingdom of God. That therefore, to the end the Sovereign King may rest on that Throne of thy Soul, thou ought to take pains to keep it clean, quiet, void and peaceable; clean from guilt and defects; quiet from fears; void of affections, desires, and thoughts; and peaceable in temptations and tribulations.

2. Thou ought always then to keep thine Heart in peace; that thou may keep pure that Temple of God, and with a right and pure intention, thou art to work, pray, obey and suffer, without being in the least moved, whatever it pleases the Lord to send unto thee. Because it is certain, that for the good of thy Soul, and for thy spiritual profit, he will suffer the envious enemy to trouble that City of Rest, and Throne of Peace, with temptations, suggestions and tribulations, and by the means of creature, with painful troubles and grievous persecutions.

3. Be constant, and cheer up thine heart in whatsoever disquiet these tribulations may cause to thee. Enter within it, that thou may overcome it;

for therein is the Divine Fortress, which defends, protects, and fights for thee. If a man hath a safe Fortress, he is not disquieted, though his enemies pursue him; because, by retreating within it, these are disappointed and overcome. The strong Castle, that will make thee triumph over all thine enemies, visible and invisible, and over all their snares and tribulations, is within thine own Soul, because in it resides the Divine Aid and Sovereign Succour. Retreat within it and all will be quiet, secure, peaceable and calm.

4. It ought to be thy chief and continual exercise, to pacifie that Throne of thy Heart that the Supreme King may rest therein. The way to pacifie it, will be, to enter into thy self by means of internal recollection; all thy protection is to be Prayer and a loving recollection in the Divine Presence. When thou seest thy self more sharply assaulted, retreat into that region of Peace, where thou'lt find the Fortress. When thou are more faint-hearted, betake thy self to this refuge of Prayer, the only Armor for overcoming the enemy, and mitigating tribulation: thou ought not to be at a distance from it in a Storm, to the end thou mayest, as another *Noah*, experience tranquility, security and serenity, and to the end thy will may be resigned, devote, peaceful and courageous.

5. Finally, be not afflicted nor discouraged to see thy self faint-hearted, he returns to quiet thee, that still he may stir thee, because this Divine Lord will be alone with thee, to rest in thy Soul, and form therein a rich Throne of Peace; that within thine own heart, by means of internal recollection, and with his heavenly Grace, thou may look for silence in tumult, solitude in company, light in darkness, forgetfulness in pressures, vigour in despondency, courage in fear, resistance in temptation, peace in war, and quiet in tribulation.

SECTION TWO: *Though the Soul perceive it self deprived of Discourse, or Ratiocination, yet it ought to presevere in Prayer, and not be afflicted, because that is its greater Felicity.*

6. Thoul't find thy self, as all other Souls that are called by the Lord to the inward way, full of confusion and doubts, because in Prayer thou hast failed in Discourse: It will seem to thee that God does no more assist thee as formerly, that the exercise of Prayer is not in thy power; that thou losest time, whilst hardly and with great trouble thou canst make one single Ejaculation as thou wast wont to do.

7. How much confusion, and what perplexities will that want of enlarging thy self in mental Discourse raise in thee? And if in such a juncture thou hast not a ghostly Father, expert in the Mystical Way, thou'lt certainly conclude that thy Soul is out of order, and that for the security of thy Conscience, thou standest in need of a general confession; and all that will be got by that care, will be the shame and confusion of both. O how

many Souls are called to the inward way, and the spiritual Fathers for want of Understanding their case, instead of guiding and helping them forwards, stop them in their Course, and ruin them.

8. Thou ought then to be perswaded, that thou may not draw back, when thou wantest expansion and discourse in Prayer; that it is thy greatest happiness, because it is a clear sign, that the Lord will have thee to walk by Faith and Silence in his Divine Presence, which is the most profitable and easiest Path; in respect, that with a simple view, or amorous attention to God, the Soul appears like a humble Supplicant before its Lord, or as an innocent Child, that casts it self into the sweet and safe Bosom of its dear Mother. Thus did Gerson express it, *Though I have spent Fourty Years in Reading and Prayer, yet I could never find any thing more efficacious, nor compendious, for attaining to Mystical Theology, than that our Spirit should become like a young Child and Beggar in the presence of God.*

9. That kind of Prayer is not only the easiest, but the most secure; because it is abstracted from the operations of the Imagination, that is always exposed to the Tricks of the Devil, and the extravagancies of Melancholy, and Ratiocination, wherein the Soul is easily Distracted, and being wrapt up in speculation, reflects on it self.

10. When God had a mind to instruct his own Captain *Moses*, and give him the two Tablets of the Law (Exod. 24.), written in Stone, he called him up to the Mountain, at what time God being there with him, the Mount was Darkened and environed with thick Clouds, *Moses* standing idle, not knowing what to think or say. Seven days after God commanded *Moses*, to come up to the top of the Mountain, where he show'd him his Glory, and filled him with great Consolation.

11. So in the Beginning, when God intends after an extraordinary manner, to guide the Soul into the School of the divine and loving Notices of the internal Law, he makes it go with Darkness, and Dryness, that he may bring it near to himself, because the Divine Majesty knows very well, that it is not by the means of ones one Ratiocination, or Industry, that a Soul draws near to him, and understands the Divine Documents; but rather by silent and humble Resignation.

12. The Patriarch *Noah* gave a great instance of this; who after he had been by all men reckoned a Fool, floating in the middle of a raging Sea, wherewith the whole World was overflowed, without Sails and Oars; and environed with wild Beasts, that were shut up in the Ark, walked by Faith alone, not knowing nor understanding what God had a mind to do with him.

13. What most concerns thee, O redeemed Soul, is Patience, not to desist from the Prayer thou art about, though thou can'st not enlarge in Discourse. Walk with firm Faith, and a holy Silence, dying in thy self, with all thy natural Industry, trusting that God who is he who is, and changes

not; neither can err, intends nothing by thy good. It is clear that he who is at dying, must needs feel it, but how well is time employed, when the Soul is dead, dumb, and resigned in the presence of God, there without any clutter or distraction, to receive the Divine Influences.

14. The Senses are not capable of divine Blessings; hence if thou would be Happy and Wise; be Silent and Believe; Suffer and have Patience; be Confident and Walk on; it concerns thee far more to hold thy Peace, and to let thy self be guided by the hand of God, than to enjoy all the Goods of this World. And though it seem to thee, that thou does nothing at all, and art idle being so Dumb and Resigned; yet it is of infinite fruit.

15. Consider the blinded Beast that turns the Wheel of the Mill, which though it see not, neither know what it does, yet does a great Work in grinding the Corn, and although it taste not of it; yet its Master receives the fruit, and tastes of the same. Who would not think, during so long a time that the Seed lies in the Earth, but that it were lost? Yet afterwards it is seen to spring up, grow and multiply. God does the same with the Soul, when he deprives it of Consideration and Ratiocination: Whil'st it thinks it does nothing, and is, in a manner undone, in time it comes to itself again, improved, disengaged, and perfect, having never hoped for so much favour.

16. Take care then that thou afflict not thy self, nor draw back, though thou can'st not enlarge thy self, and discourse in Prayer; suffer, hold thy peace, and appear in the presence of God; persevere constantly, and trust to his infinite Bounty, who can give unto thee constant Faith, true light, and divine Grace. Walk as if thou were blindfolded, without thinking or reasoning; put thy self into his kind and paternal hands, resolving to do nothing but what his divine Will and Pleasure is.

SECTION THREE: *A Sequel of the same Matter.*

17. It is the common opinion of all the holy Men who have treated of the Spirit, and of all the Mystical Matters: That the Soul cannot attain to perfection and an union with God, by means of Meditation, and Ratiocination: Because that is only good for beginning the spiritual Way, to the end one may acquire a habit of Knowledg, of the beauty of Vertue, and ugliness of Vice: which habit in the opinion of Saint Teresa, may be attained to in Six Months time and according to S. Bonaventure (In prolp. de Mist. Theol. page 655) in two.

18. O how are, in a manner infinite numbers of Souls to be pitied, who from the beginning of their Life to the end, employ themselves in meer Meditation, constraining themselves to Reason, although God Almighty deprive them of Ratiocination, that he may promote them to another State, and carry them on a more perfect kind of Prayer, and so for many years they continue imperfect, and in the beginning, without any progress or

having as yet made one step in the way of the Spirit; beating their Brains about the frame of the Place, the choice of the Minutes, Imaginations, and strained Reasonings, seeking God without, when in the mean time, they have him within themselves.

19. St. Austin (Soliloq. C. 31) complained of that, in the time when God led him to the Mystical Way, saying to his Divine Majestie, *I, Lord, went wandering like a strayed Sheep, seeking thee with anxious Reasoning without, whil'st thou wast within me, I wearied my self much in looking for thee without and yet thou hast thy habitation within me; If I long and breathe after thee, I went round the Streets and Places of the City of this World, seeking thee and found thee not; because, in vain I sought without for him, what was within my self.*

20. The Angelical Doctor St. Thomas, for all he was so circumspect in his Writings, may seem yet to jeer those, who go always in search of God, without by means of Ratiocination, when they have him present within themselves. *There is great Blindness, and excessive Folly in some,* (says the Saint - Ocuse. 6. C. 3. infin.) *who always seek God, continually sigh after God, often long for God, invocate and call upon God daily in Prayer; they themselves (according to the Apostle) being the living Temple of God, and his true Habitation, since their Soul is the Seat and Throne of God, where he continually rests. Who then, but a Fool, will look for an Instrument abroad, when he knows he has it fast shut up within Doors? Or who can refresh himself with the Food he desires, and yet not taste it? Such exactly is the Live of some just men, always seeking, and never enjoying, and therefore all their Works are imperfect.*

21. It is certain, that Our *Lord Christ* taught Perfection to all, and ever will have all to be Perfect, particularly the Ignorant and Simple. He clearly manifested this Truth, when for his Apostles, he chose the Smallest and most Ignorant, saying (Matth. II.) to his Eternal Father, *I thank thee, O Father, Lord of Heaven and Earth, because thou hast hid these things from the Wise and Prudent, and hast revealed them unto Babes.* And it is certain, that these cannot acquire Perfection, by acute Meditations, and subtle Reasonings, though they be as capable as the most Learned, to attain to Perfection, by the affections of the Will, wherein principally it consists.

22. St. Bonaventure, teaches us not to form Conceptions of any thing, no not of God, because it is Imperfection to make Representations, Images, and Ideas, how subtle or ingenious soever, either of the Will, or of the Goodness, Trinity, and Unity; nay, of the Divine Presence it self: In respect that, though all these Representations appear *Deiform*, yet are they not God, who admits of no Image, nor Form. *Non ibi* (says the Saint - Mist. Theol. p.2., Vn. p. 685.) *oportet cogitare res de creaturis nec de, Angelis, nec de Trinitate, quia hæc sapientia per affectus desideriorum, non per meditationem,* præviam *debet consurgere.* We must not here think any thing of Creature, of Angles, nor of God himself, because that Wisdom and Perfection, is not acquired by nice and quaint Meditation, but by the desire and affection of the Will.

23. The holy man cannot speak more clearly; and thou would'st disquiet they self, and leave off Prayer, because thou know'st not, or can'st not tell how to enlarge therein, though thou may'st have a good Will, good Desire, and pure Intention? If the young Ravens forsaken of the old, because seeing them without Black Feathers, they think them Spurious, are by the Dew of Heaven fed that they may not perish; what will he do to redeem Souls, though they cannot speak nor reason, if they believe, trust, and open their Mouths to Heaven, declaring their wants: It is not more certain that the Divine Bounty will provide for them, and give them their necessary Food?

24. Manifest it is, that it is a great Martyrdom, and no small Gift of God, for the Soul, finding it self deprived of the sensible Pleasures it had, to walk by holy Faith only, through the dark, and desart Paths of Perfection, to which, notwithstanding, it can never attain but by this painful, though secure means. Wherefore endeavour to be constant, and not draw back, though Discourse be wanting to thee in Prayer, believe at that time firmly, be quietly silent, and patiently persevere if thou wouldest be happy, and attain to the Divine Union, eminent rest, and to the Supream Internal Peace.

SECTION FOUR: *The Soul is not to afflict it self, nor intermit Prayer, because it sees it self encompassed with dryness.*

25. Thou shalt know that there are two sorts of Prayer, the one tender, delightful, amicable, and full of sentiments; the other obscure, dry, desolate, tempted, and darksome. The first is of Beginners, the second of Proficients, who are in the progress to Perfection. God gives the first to gain Souls, the second to purifie them. With the first he uses them like Children; with the second he begins to deal with them as with strong men.

26. This first Way may be called the Animal Life, and belongs to them who go in the tract of the sensible Devotion, which God uses to give to Beginners, to the end that being endowed with that small relish, as the natural man is with the sensible Object, they may addict themselves to the spiritual Life. The second is called the Life of men, and belongs to those, who not minding sensible Pleasures, fight and war against their own Passions, that they may conquer and obtain Perfection, the proper employment of men.

27. Assure thy self, that dryness or aridity is the Instrument of thy Good, because it is nothing else but a want of sensibility, that Remora, which puts a stop to the flight of almost all Spiritual Men, and makes them even draw back, and leave off Prayer: as may be seen in many Souls, which only persevere whil'st they taste sensible Consolation.

28. Know that the Lord makes use of the Veil of Dryness, to the end we

may not know what he is working in us, and so be humble; because if we felt and knew what he is working in our Souls, satisfaction and presumption would get in, imagining that we were doing some good thing, and reckoning our selves very near to God; which would be our undoing.

29. Lay this down as a firm ground in thine Heart, that for walking in the inward Way, all sensibilitie should first be removed; and that the means God uses for that is driness. By that also he takes away reflection, or that view, whereby the Soul Eyes what it is doing, the only impediment that obstructs the advancing forward, and God communicating himself, and operating in it.

30. Thou oughtest not then to afflict thy self, nor think that thou reapest no fruit, because in coming from a Communion or Prayer, thou hast not the experience of many sentiments, since that is a manifest Cheat. The Husbandman Sows in one time and Reaps in another: So God, upon occasions, and in his own due time, will help them to resist Temptations, and when least thou thinkest, will give thee holy purposes, and more effectual desires of serving him. And to the end , thou mayest not suffer thy self to be transported, by the violent suggestion of the Enemy, who will enviously perswade thee, that thou do'st nothing, and that thou losest time, that so thou mayest neglect Prayer: I'll declare to thee some of the infinite fruits, that thy Soul reaps from that great dryness.

31. The first is to persevere in Prayer, from which fruit springs many other advantages.

II. Thou'lt find a loathing of the things of the World, which by little and little tends to the stifling of the bad desires of thy past Life, and the production of other new ones of serving God.

III. Thou'lt reflect upon many failings on which formerly thou didst not reflect.

IV. Thou'lt find, when thou are about to commit any evil, an advertency in thy Heart, which restrains thee from the execution of it, and at other times from Speaking. Lamenting, or Revenging thy self; that'll take thee off from some little earthy Pleasure, or from this or t'other Occasion, or Conversation, into which formerly thou was running in great Peace and Security, without the least Check or Remorse of Conscience.

V. After that through frailty, thou hast fallen in to some light fault, thou'lt feel a Reproof for it in thy Soul, which will exceeding afflict thee.

VI. Thou'lt feel within thy self, desires of suffering, and of doing the will of God.

VII. An inclination to Virtue, and greater ease in overcoming thy self, and conquering the difficulties of the Passions, and Enemies that hinder thee in the way.

VIII. Thoul't know thy self better, and be confounded also in thy self, feel in thee a high esteem of God above all created Beings, a contempt of

Creatures, and a firm Resolution not to abandon Prayer, though thou knowest that it will prove to thee a most cruel Martyrdom.

IX. Thou't be sensible of greater Peace in thy Soul, love to Humility, confidence in God, submission, and abstraction from all Creatures; and finally the Sins thou hast omitted since the time that thou exercised thy self in Prayer, are so many signs, that the Lord is working in thy Soul, (though thou knowest it not) by means of dry Prayer; and although thou feelest it not whilst thou art in prayer, thou't feel it in his due time, when he shall think it fit.

32. All these and many other fruits are like new Buds that spring from the Prayer, which thou would'st give over, because it seems to thee to be dry, that thou seest no Fruit of it, nor reapest no advantage therefrom. Be constant and persevere with Patience, for though thou knowest it not, thy Soul is profited thereby.

SECTION FIVE: *Treating of the same thing, declaring how many ways of Devotion there are, and how the sensible Devotion is to be disposed; and that the Soul is not idle, though it reason not.*

33. There are to be found two sorts of Devotion, the one essential and true; the other accidental and sensible. The essential, is a promptitude of mind to do well, (1) (*S.Thom.2.2.q.82.art.I.*) fulfil the commands of God, and to perform all things belonging to his service, though, through humane frailty, all be not actually done as is desired. (2) (*Suar.t.2.de.Pel.l.2.c.6.n.16&18.*) This is true Devotion, though it be not accompanied with pleasure, sweetness, delight, nor tears, but rather it is usually attended with temptation, dryness, and darkness.

34. Accidental and sensible Devotion is, (3) (*St.Bern.Ser.I.de Nat.Dom.Suarez in Molin de Oration. c.6.*) when good desires are attended with a pleasant softness of heart, tenderness of tears, or other sensible affections. This is not to be sought after, nay, it is rather more secure to wean the will from it, and to set light by it; because besides that it is usually dangerous, it is a great obstacle to progress, and the advancement in the internal way. And therefore we ought only to embrace the true and essential Devotion, which is always in our power to come by, seeing every one doing his duty may with the assistance of the Divine Grace acquire it. And this may be had with God, with Christ, with the Mysteries, with the Virgin, and with the Saints.

35. Some think that when Devotion and sensible Pleasure are given them, they are Favours of God, that thence forward they have him, and that the whole life is to be spent in breathing after that delight; but it is a cheat, because it is no more, but a consolation of nature, and a pure reflexion, wherewith the Soul beholds what it does, and hinders the doing, or

possibility of doing any thing, the acquisition of the true light, and the making of one step in the way of perfection. The Soul is a pure Spirit and is not felt; and so the internal acts, and of the will, as being the acts of the Soul and spiritual, are not sensible: Hence the Soul knows not if it liveth, nor, for most part, is sensible if it acteth.

36. From this thou mayest infer, that that Devotion and sensible Pleasure, is not God, not Spirit, but the product of Nature; that therefore thou oughtest to set light by, and despise it, but firmly to persevere in Prayer, leaving thy self to the conduct of God, who will be to thee light in aridity and darkness.

37. Think not that when thou art dry and darksom in the presence of God, with faith and silence, that thou do'st nothing, that thou losest time, and that thou are idle, because not to wait on God, according to the saying of St. Bernard (*Tom.5.in Fract. de vit. solit.c.8.p. 90.*), is the greatest idleness: *Otiosum non est vacare Deo; inimo negotiorum omnium hoc est*; And elsewhere he sayeth, that that idleness of the Soul is the business of the businesses of God. *Hoc negotium magnum est negotium.*

38. It is not to be said, that the Soul is idle; because though it operate not *Actively*, yet the Holy Ghost operates in it. Besides, that it is not without all activity, because it operates, though spiritually, simply, and intimately. For to be attentive to God, draw near to him, to follow his internal inspirations, receive his divine influences, adore him in his own intimate center, reverence him with the pious affections of the will, to cast away so many and so fantastical imaginations, and with softness and contempt to overcome so many temptations: all these, I say, are true acts though simple, wholly spiritual, & in a manner imperceptible, through the great tranquility, wherewith the Soul exerts them.

SECTION SIX: *The Soul is not to be disquieted, that is sees it self encompassed with darkness, because that is an instrument of its greater felicity.*

39. There are two sorts of darkness : some unhappy, and others happy : the first are such as arise from sin, and are unhappy, because they lead the Christian to an eternal precipice. The second are those which the Lord suffers to be in the Soul, to ground and settle it in virtue; and these are happy, because they enlighten it, fortifie it, and cause greater light therein, so that thou oughtest not to grieve and disturb thy self, nor be disconsolate in seeing thy self obscure and darksom, judging that God hath failed thee, and the light also that thou formerly had the experience of; thou oughtest rather at that time persevere constantly in Prayer, it being a manifest sign, that God of his infinite mercy intends to bring thee into the inward path, and happy way of Paradise. O how happy wilt thou be, if thou embrace it with peace and resignation, as the instrument of perfect quiet, true light, &

of all thy spiritual good.

40. Know then that the streightest, most perfect and secure way of proficients, is the way of darkness: because in them the Lord placed his own Throne; And (Psalm 18.) He made darkness his secret place. By them the supernatural light which God infuses into the Soul, grow and increases. Amidst them wisdom and strong love are begotten, by darkness the soul is annihilated, and the *species*, which hinder the right view of the divine truth, are consumed. By this means God introduces the Soul by the inward way into the Prayer of Rest, and of perfect contemplation, which so few have the experience of. Finally; by darkness the Lord purgest the senses and sensibility, which hinder the mystical progress.

41. See now if darkness be not to be esteemed and embraced. What thou oughtest to do amidst them, is to believe, that thou art before the Lord, and in his Presence; but thou oughtest to do so, with a sweet and quiet attention; not desire to know any thing, nor search after delicacies, tenderness or sensible devotions, nor do any thing but what is the good will and pleasure of God; Because otherwise thou wilt only make circles, all thy life time, and not advance one step toward perfection.

SECTION SEVEN: *To the end the Soul may attain to the supreme internal peace, it is necessary, that God purge it after his way, because the exercises and mortifications that of it self it sets about, are not sufficient.*

42. So soon as thou shalt firmly resolve to mortifie thy external senses, that thou may'st advance towards the high mountain of perfection, and union with God; His divine Majesty will set his hand to the purging of thy evil inclinations, inordinate desires, vain complacency, self-love and pride, and other hidden vices, which thou knowest not, and yet reign in the inner parts of thy Soul, and hinder the divine union.

43. Thou'lt never attain to this happy state, though thou tire thy self out with the external acts of mortifications and resignation, until this Lord purge thee inwardly, and discipline thee, after his own way, because he alone knows how secret faults are to be purged out. If thou persevere constantly, he'll not only purge thee from affections and engagements to natural and temporal goods, but in his own time also he will purifie thee with the supernatural and sublime, such as are internal communications; inward raptures and extasies, and other infused graces, on which the Soul rests and enjoys it self.

44. God will do all this in thy Soul by means of the cross, and dryness, if thou freely giveth thy consent to it by resignation, and walking through those darksom and desart ways. All thou hast to do, is to do nothing by thy own choice alone. The subjection of thy liberty, is that which thou oughtest to do, quietly resigning thy self up in every thing whereby the Lord shall

think fit internally and externally to mortifie thee: because that is the only means, by which thy Soul can become capable of the divine influences, whil'st thou sufferest internal and external tribulation, with humility, patience, and quiet; not the penances, disciplines and mortifications, which thou couldest impose upon thy self.

45. The husbandman sets a greater esteem upon the plants which he sows in the ground, than those that spring up of themselves, because these never come to seasonable maturity. In the same manner God esteems and is better pleased with the vertue, which he sows and infuses into the Soul (as being sunk into its own nothingness, calm and quiet, retreated within its own center, and without any election) than all the other vertues which the Soul pretends to acquire by its own election and endeavours.

46. It concerns thee only then, to prepare thine heart, like clean paper, wherein the divine wisdom may imprint characters to his own liking. O how great a work will it be for thy Soul to be whole hours together in Prayer, dumb, resigned, and humble, without acting, knowing, or desiring to understand any thing.

SECTION EIGHT: *A Sequel of the same.*

47. With new efforts thoul't exercise thy self, but in another manner than hitherto, giving thy consent to receive the secret and divine operations, and to be polished, and purified by this Lord, which is the only means whereby thou will become clean & purged from thine ignorance and dissolutions. Know, however, that thou art to be plunged in a bitter sea of sorrows, and of internal and external pains, which torment will pierce into the most inward part of thy Soul and Body.

48. Thoul't experience, that the creatures will forsake thee, nay, those too from which thou hoped'st for most favour and compassion in thy streights; the brooks of thy faculties will be so dried up, that thou shalt' not be able to form any ratiocination, nay, nor so much as to conceive a good thought of God. Heaven will seem to thee to be of brass, and thou shalt receive no light from it. Nor will the thought comfort thee, that in times past so much light and devote consolation have rained into thy Soul.

49. The invisible enemies will pursue thee with scruples, lascivious suggestions, and unclean thoughts, with incentives to impatience, pride, rage, cursing and blaspheming the Name of God, his Sacraments, and holy Mysteries. Thou'lt find a great lukewarmness, loathing, and wearisomness for the things of God; and obscurity and darkness in thy understanding; a faintness, Confusion and narrowness of heart; such a coldness and feebleness of the will to resist, that a straw will appear to thee a beam. Thy desertion will be so great, that thou'lt think there is no more a God for thee, and that thou are rendered incapable of entertaining a good desire: so

that thou'lt continue shut up betwixt two walls, in constant streights and anguish, without any hopes of ever getting out of so dreadful an oppression.

50. But fear not: all this is necessary for purging thy Soul, and making it know its own misery, and sensibly perceive the annihilation of all the passions, and disordinate appetites, wherewith it rejoyced it self. Finally, to the end the Lord may refine and purifie thee after his own manner with those inward torments, wilt thou not cast the *Jonas* of sense into the sea, that thereby thou mayest procure it? With all thy outward disciplines and mortifications, thou'lt never have true light, nor make one step towards perfection: so that thou wilt stop in the beginning, and thy Soul will not attain to the amiable rest, and supream internal peace.

SECTION NINE: *The Soul ought not to be disquieted, nor draw back in the spiritual way, because it finds it self assaulted by temptations.*

51. Our own nature is so base, proud and ambitious, and so full of its own appetites, its own judgements and opinions, that if temptations restrained it not, it would be undone without remedy. The Lord then seeing our Misery and perverse inclination, and thereby moved to compassion, suffers us to be assaulted by divers thoughts against the Faith, horrible temptations, and by violent and painful suggestions of impatience, pride, gluttony, luxury, rage, blasphemy, cursing, despair, and an infinite number of others, to the end we may know our selves and be humble. With these horrible temptations, that infinite goodness humbles our pride, giving us in them the most wholesome medicine.

52. All our righteousness (as Isaiah saith) are as filthy rags, (Chap. 64. 6.) through the stains of vanity, conceitedness, and self-love. It is necessary they be purified with the fire of tribulation and temptation, that so they may be clean, pure, perfect and agreeable to the eyes of God.

53. Therefore the Lord purifies the Soul which he calls, and will have for himself, with the rough file of temptation, with which he polishes it from the rust of pride, avarice, vanity, ambition, presumption, and self-conceitedness. With the same, he humbles, pacifies and exercises it, making it to know its own misery. By means thereof he purifies and strips the heart to the end all its operations may be pure, and inestimable value.

54. Many Souls when they suffer these painful torments, are troubled, afflicted, and disquieted, it seeming to them, that they begin already in this life to suffer eternal punishments; and if by misfortune they go to an unexperienced Confessor, instead of comforting them, he leaves them in greater confusion and perplexities.

55. That thou mayest not lose internal peace, it is necessary thou believe, that it is the goodness of divine mercy, when thus it humbles, afflicts and

trys thee; since by that means thy Soul comes to have a deep knowledge of itself, reckoning it self the worst, most impious and abominable of all Souls living, and hence with humility and lowliness it abhors it self. O how happy would Souls be, if they would be quiet and believe, that all these temptations are caused by the Devil, and received from the hand of God, for their gain and spiritual profit.

56. But thou'lt say, that it is not the work of the Devil, when he molests thee by means of creatures, but the effect of thy neighbours fault and malice, in having wronged and injured thee. Know that that is another cunning and hidden temptation, because though God wills not the sin of another, yet he wills his own effect in thee, and the trouble which accrues to thee from another's fault, that he may see thee emproved by the benefit of patience.

57. Doest thou receive an injury from any man? there are two things in it, the sin of him that does it, and the punishment that thou sufferest; the sin is against the will of God, and displeases him, though he permit it; the punishment is conform to his will, and he wills it for thy good, wherefore thou oughtest to receive it, as from his hand. The Passion and Death of our Lord Christ, were the effects of the wickedness and sins of *Pilate*, and yet it is certain, that God willed the death of his own Son for our redemption.

58. Consider how the Lord makes use of another's fault for the good of thy Soul. O the greatness of the Divine Wisdom, who can pry into the depth of the secret and extraordinary means, and the hidden paths whereby he guides the Soul, which he would have purged, transformed and deified.

SECTION TEN: *Wherein the Same Point is Handled*

59. That the Soul may be the habitation of the celestial King, it is necessary, that it should be pure and without any blemish; wherefore the Lord purifies it as gold in the furnace of terrible and grievous temptations. Certain it is, that the Soul never loves, nor believes more, than when it is afflicted and baited with such temptations; because those doubtings and fears that beset it, whether it believe or not; whether it consent or not, are nothing else but the quaintnesses of love.

60. The effects that remain in the Soul make this very clear; and commonly these are a loathing of it self with a most profound acknowledgment of the greatness and omnipotence of God, a great confidence in the Lord, that he will deliver it from all risk and danger; believing and confessing with far greater vigour of faith, that it is God who gives it strength to bear the torments of these temptations, because it would naturally be impossible, considering the force and violence wherewith sometimes they attack, to resist one quarter of an hour.

61. Thou art to know then, that temptation is thy great happiness, so

that the more it besets thee, the more thou oughtest to rejoyce in Peace, instead of being sad, and thank God for the favour he does thee. In all these temptations, and odious thoughts, the remedy that is to work, is to despise them with a stayed neglect, because nothing more afflicts the proud Devil, than to see that he is slighted and despised, as are all things else that he suggests to us. And therefore thou art to tarry with him, as one that perceives him not, and to possess thy self in thy peace without repining, and without multiplying Reasons and Answers; seeing nothing is more dangerous, than to vie in reasons with him who is ready to deceive thee.

62. The Saints in arriving at holiness, passed through this doleful valley of temptation, and the greater Saints they were the greater temptations they grapled with. Nay after the Saints have attained to holiness and perfection; the Lord suffers them to be tempted with brisk temptations, that their Crown may be the greater, and that the spirit of Vain-glory may be checked, or else hindred from entring in them, keeping them in that manner secure, humble, and sollicitous of their condition.

63. Finally thou art to know, that the greatest Temptation is to be without Temptation; wherefore thou oughtest to be glad when it assaults thee, and with Resignation, Peace and Constancy resist it: Because if thou wilt serve God, and arrive at the sublime Region of Internal Peace; thou must pass through that rugged Path of Temptation; put on that heavy Armor; fight in that fierce and cruel War, and in that burning Furnace, polish, purge, renew, and purifie thy self.

SECTION ELEVEN: *Declaring the Nature of internal Recollection, and instructing the Soul how it ought to behave it self therein, and in the Spiritual Welfare, whereby the Devil endeavours to disturb it at that time.*

64. Internal Recollection is Faith, and Silence in the Presence of God. Hence thou oughtest to be accustomed to recollect thy self in his Presence, with an affectionate attention, as one that is given up to God, and united unto him, with Reverence, Humility and Submission, beholding him in the most inward recess of thine own Soul, without Form, Likeness, Manner, or Figure; in the view and general nature of a loving and obscure Faith, without any distinction of Perfection or Attribute.

65. There thou art to be with attention, and a sincere regard, with a sedate heedfulness, and full of Love towards the same Lord, resigning and delivering thy self up into his hands, to the end he may dispose of thee, according to his good Will and Pleasure; without reflecting on thy self; nay, nor on Perfection it self. Here thou art to shut up the Senses, trusting God with all the care of thy Welfare, and minding nothing of the affairs this Life. Finally, thy Faith ought to be pure, without Representations or Likeness: Simple without Reasonings, and Universal without Distinctions.

66. The Prayer of Internal Recollection may be well typified by that Wrestling, which the holy Scripture says, the Patriarch *Jacob* had all Night with God, until Day broke, and he Blessed him. Wherefore the Soul is to persevere, and wrestle with the difficulties that it will find in internal Recollection, without desisting, until the Son of internal Light begin to appear, and the Lord give it his Blessing.

67. No sooner wilt thou have given thy self up to thy Lord in this inward Way, but all Hell will conspire against thee, seeing one single Soul inwardly retired to its own Presence, makes greater War against the Enemy, than a thousand others that walk externally; because the Devil makes an infinite advantage of an internal Soul.

68. In the time of the recollection, Peace and Resignation of thy Soul, God will more esteem the various impertinent, troublesome and ugly thoughts that thou hast, than the good purposes, and high sentiments. Know that the effort, which thou thy self mayest make to resist Thoughts, is an impediment, and will leave thy Soul in greater anxitie. The best thing that is to be done, is sweetly to dispise them, to know thine own wretchedness, and peacefully make an Offering to God of the Trouble.

69. Though thou canst not get rid of the anguish of Thoughts, hast no Light, Comfort, nor spiritual Sentiment: Yet be not afflicted, neither leave off recollection, because they are the Snares of the Enemy: Resign thy self at the time with Vigour, endure with Patience, and persevere in his Presence; for whil'st thou perseverest after that manner, thy Soul will be internally emproved.

70. Doest thou believe that when thou comest away from Prayer dry, in the same manner as thou began it; that that was because of want of Preparation, and that hath done thee no good: That is a Fallacy: Because the fruit of true Prayer consists not in enjoying the Light, nor in having Knowledge of spiritual things, since these may be found in a speculative Intellect, without true Virtue and Perfection; it only consists in enduring with Patience, and persevering in Faith and Silence, believing that thou art in the Lord's Presence, turning to him thy Heart with tranquillity, and purity of Mind. So whilst thou perseversest in this manner, thou'lt have the only Preparation and disposition which at that time is necessary, and shalt reap infinite fruit.

71. War is very usual in this internal Recollection, which on the one hand will deprive thee of sensibility, to try, humble, and purge thee. On the other, invisible Enemies will assault thee with continual Suggestions, to trouble and disquiet thee. Nature her self, apparently, will torment thee, she being always an Enemy to the Spirit, which in depriving her of sensible Pleasures, remains Weak, Melancholy, and full of Irksomness, so that it feels a Hell in all Spiritual Exercises, particularly in that of Prayer, hence it grows extreamly impatient to be at an end of it, through the uneasiness of

Thoughts, the lassitude of Body, importunate Sleep, and the not being able to curb the Senses, every one of which would for it own share, follow its own Pleasure. Happy art thou if thou canst persevere amidst this Martyrdom!

74. That great Doctoress, and Mystical Mistress, Santa Teresa, confirms all this by her heavenly Doctrine, in the Letter she wrote to the Bishop of Osmia, to instruct him, how he was to behave himself in Prayer, and in the variety of troublesome thoughts, which attack us at that time, where she says (8. Of her Epistolary.): *There is a necessity of suffering the trouble of a Troop of Thoughts, importune Imaginations, and the impetuosities of natural Notions, not only, of the Soul through the dryness and disunion it hath, but of the Body also, occasioned by the want of submission to the Spirit, which it ought to have.*

73. These are called drynesses in Spirituals, but are very profitable, if they be embraced and suffered with Patience. Who so shall accustom himself to suffer them without repining, will from that labour draw vast advantage. It is certain, that in recollection the Devil frequently charges the Soul more fiercely with a Battalion of Thoughts, to discomfit the quiet of the Soul, and alienate it from that most sweet and secure internal Conversation, raising horrours, to the end it may leave it off, reducing it most commonly to such a state, as if it were lead forth to a most rigorous Torment.

74. The Birds, which are the Devils, knowing this (said the Saint in the above cited Letter) pricks and molest the Soul with Imaginations, troublesome Thoughts, and the Interruptions which the Devil at that time brings in, transporting the Thought, distracting it from one thing to another, and after he hath done with them attacking the Heart, and it is no small fruit of Prayer, patiently to suffer these Troubles and Importunities. That is an offering up of ones self, in a whole burnt Sacrifice, that's to say, to be wholly consumed in the Fire of Temptation, and no part spared. See, how this heavenly Mistress encourages to suffer and endure Thoughts and Temptations; because, provided they be not consented to, they double the profit.

75. As many times as thou exercisest thy self, calmly to reject these vain Thoughts, so many Crowns will the Lord set upon thy Head, and though it may seem to thee that thou dost nothing, be undeceiv'd, for a good desire with firmness and stedfastness in Prayer, is very pleasing to the Lord.

76. Wherefore to be there (concludes the Saint) without sensible profit, is not lost time; but of great gain, whil'st one toyls without Interest, and meerly for the glory of God; and though it may seem to be toyling in vain, yet it is not so, but it is as with Children, who toyl and labour under the power of their Father: though in the evening they receive not the wages for their day's work, yet at the year's end they enjoy all. In fine, you see how the saint confirms our document with her precious doctrine.

SECTION TWELVE: *A Sequel of the Same Matter*

77. God loves not him who does most, who hears most, nor who shows greatest affection, but who suffers most, if he pray with faith and reverence, believing that he is in the divine presence. The truth is to take from the Soul the prayer of the Senses, and of Nature, is a rigorous martyrdom to it, but the Lord rejoyces, and is glad in its peace, if it be thus quiet and resigned. Use not at that time vocal Prayer, because however it be good and holy in it self, yet to use it then, is a manifest temptation, whereby the enemy pretends, that God speaks not to thy heart, under pretext that thou had not sentiments, and that thou losest time.

78. God hath no regard to the multitude of words, but to the purity of the intent. His greatest content and glory at that time, is to see the Soul in silence, desirous, humble, quiet, and resigned. Proceed, persevere, pray, and hold thy peace; for where thou findest not a sentiment, thou'lt find a door whereby thou mayest enter into thine own nothingness; knowing thy self to be nothing, that thou can'st do nothing, nay, and that thou hast not so much as a good thought.

79. How many have begun this happy practice of Prayer, and Internal Recollection, and have left it off, pretending that they feel no pleasure, that they lose time, that their thoughts trouble them, and that that Prayer is not for them, whil'st they find not any sentiment of God, nor any ability to reason or discourse; whereas they might have believed, been silent, and had patience. All this is no more, but with ingratitude to hunt after sensible pleasures, suffering themselves to be transported with self-love, seeking themselves, and not God, because they cannot suffer a little pain and dryness, without reflecting on the infinite loss they sustain, whereas by the least act of reverence towards God, amidst dryness and sterility, they receive an eternal reward.

80. The Lord told the venerable Mother Francesca Lopez of Valenza, and a religious of the third Order of St. *Francis*, three things of great light and consequence in order to internal recollection. *In the first place, that a quarter of an hour of Prayer, with recollection of the senses and faculties, and with resignation and humility, does more good to the Soul than five days of penitential exercises, hair cloaths, disciplines, fastings, and sleeping on bare boards, because these are only mortifications of the body, and with recollection the Soul is purified.*

81. Secondly, That it is more pleasing to the Divine Majesty, to have the Soul in quiet and devote Prayer for the space of an hour, than to go in great Pilgrimages; because that in Prayer it does good to it self, and to those for whom it prays, gives delight to God, and merits a high degree of glory, but in pilgrimage, commonly, the Soul is distracted, and the Senses diverted, with a debilitation of vertue, besides many other dangers.

82. Thirdly, That constant Prayer was to keep the Heart always right towards God, and that a Soul to be internal, ought rather to act with the affection of the Will, than the toyl of the Intellect. All this is to be read in her Life.

83. The more the Soul rejoyces in sensible love, the less delight God has in it; on the contrary, the less the Soul rejoyces in this sensible love, the more God delights in it. And know that to fix the Will on God, restraining thoughts and temptations, with the greatest tranquillity possible, is the highest pitch of Praying.

84. I'll conclude this Chapter by undeceiving thee of the vulgar errour of those who say, that in this internal Recollection, or Prayer of Rest, the faculties operate not, and that the Soul is idle and wholly unactive. This is a manifest fallacy of those who have little experience, because although it operate not by means of the memory, nor by the second operation of the Intellect, which is the judgment, nor by the third, which is discourse or ratiocination, yet it operates by the first and chief operation of the intellect, which is simple apprehension, enlightened by holy Faith, and aided by the divine gifts of the holy Spirit. And the Will is more apt to continue one act, than to multiply many; so that as well the act of the Intellect, as that of the Will are so simple, imperceptible, and spiritual, that hardly the Soul knows them, and far less reflects upon them.

SECTION THIRTEEN: What the Soul ought to do in Internal Recollection

85. Thou oughtest to go to Prayer, that thou mayest deliver thy self wholly up into the hands of God, with perfect resignation, exerting an act of Faith, believing that thou art in the divine Presence, afterwards setling in that holy repose, with quietness, silence and tranquility; and endeavouring for a whole day, a whole year, and thy whole life to continue that first act of Contemplation, by faith and love.

86. It is not your businesses to multiply these acts, nor to repeat sensible affections, because they hinder the Purity of the spiritual and perfect act of the Will, whil'st besides that these sweet sentiments are imperfect, (considering the reflection wherewith they are made, the self-content, and external consolation wherewhith they are fought after, the Soul being drawn outwards to the external faculties) there is no necessity of renewing them, as the mystical *Falcon* hath excellently expressed it by the following similitude.

87. If a Jewel given to a friend were once put into his hands, it is not necessary to repeat such a donation already made, by daily telling him, (Sir, I give you that Jewel, Sir, I give you that Jewel), but to let him keep it, and not take it from him, because provided he take it not, or design not to take it from him, he hath surely given it him.

88. In the same manner, having once dedicated, and lovingly resign thy self to the will of God, there is nothing else for thee to do, but to continue the same, without repeating new and sensible acts, provided thou takest not back the Jewel thou hast once given, by committing some notable fault against his divine Will, tho thou oughtest still to exercise thy self outwardly in the external works of thy calling and state, for in so doing thou dost the Will of God, and walkest in continual and virtual oration: *He always prays* (said *Theophylact*) *who does good works, nor does he neglect Prayer, but when he leaves off to be just.*

89. Thou oughtest then to slight all those sensibilities, to the end thy Soul may be established, and acquire a habit of internal recollection which is so effectual, that the resolution only of going to Prayer, awakens a lively presence of God, which is the preparation to the Prayer that is about to be made; or to say better, is no other than a more efficacious continuation of continual Prayer, wherein the contemplative person ought to be settled.

90. O how well did the venerable Mother of Cantal, the spiritual daughter of St. *Francis* of *Sales*, practice this Lesson, in whole Life are the following words, written to her Master: *Most dear Father, I cannot do any act, it seems to me always that this is the most firm and secure disposition: my spirit in the upper part, is in a most simple unity; it is not united, because when it would perform acts of union (which it often sets about) it finds difficulty, and clearly perceives that it cannot unite, but be united. The Soul would make use of this union, for the service of Mattins, the holy Mass, preparation for the Communion, and thanksgiving; and in a word, it would for all things be always in that most simple unity of spirit, without reflecting on any thing else.* To all this the holy Father answered with approbation, perswading her to persist, and putting her in mind, that the repose of God is in peace.

91. Another time she wrote to the same Saint these words: Endeavouring to do some more special acts of my simple intuition, total resignation and annihilation in God, his divine goodness rebuked me, and gave me to understand, that that proceeded only from the love of my self, and that thereby I offended my Soul.

92. By this thou wilt be undeceived, and know what is the perfect and spiritual way of Praying, and be advised what is to be done in Internal recollection: Thou'lt know that to the end Love may be perfect and pure, it is expedient to retrench the multiplication of sensible and fervent Acts, the Soul continuing quiet and resting in that inward Silence. Because, tenderness, delight, and sweet sentiments, which the Soul experiences in the Will, are not pure Spirits, but Acts blended with the sensibility of Nature. Nor is it perfect Love, but sensible Pleasure, which distracts and hurts the Soul, as the Lord told the venerable Mother of *Cantal*.

93. How happy and how well applied will thy Soul be, if retreating within it self, it there shrink into its own nothing, both in its Center and superiour Part, without minding what it does; whether it recollect or not,

whether it walk well or ill; if it operate or not, without heeding, thinking, or minding any sensible thing? At that time the Intellect believes with a pure Act, and the Will loves with perfect love, without any kind of impediment, imitating that pure and continued Act of Intuition and Love, which the Saints say the Blessed in Heaven have, with no other difference, than that they see one another there Fact to Face, and the Soul here, through the Veil of an obscure Faith.

94. O how few are the Souls, that attain to this perfect way of Praying, because they penetrate not enough into this internal recollection, and Mystical Silence, and because they strip not themselves of imperfect reflection, and sensible pleasure! O that thy Soul, without thoughtful advertency, even of it self, might give it self in Prey to that holy and spiritual Tranquility, and say with St. Austin (*In his Confess. lib. 9. cap. 10.*), *Sileat anima mea, & transeat se, non se cogitando!* Let it be silent and do nothing, forget it self, and plung into that obscure Faith: How secure and safe would it be, though it might seem to it that thus unactive and doing nothing it were undone.

95. I'll sum up this doctrine with a Letter that the Illuminated Mother of Cantal wrote to a Sister, and great Servant of God: *Divine Bounty* (said she) *granted me this way of Prayer, that with a single View of God, I felt my self wholly dedicated to him, absorpt and reposed in him; he still continued to me that Grace, though I opposed it by my Infidelity, giving way to fear, and thinking my self unprofitable in that state; for which cause, being willing to do something on my part, I quite spoil all; and to this present I find my self sometimes assaulted by the same Fear, though not in Prayer, but in other Exercises wherein I am always willing to employ my self a little, though I know very well, that in doing such acts, I come out of my Center, and see particularly that that simple View of God, is my only remedy and help still, in all troubles, temptations, and the events of this Life.*

96. And certainly, would I have followed my internal Impulse, I should have made use of no other means in any thing whatsoever, without exception; because when I think to fortifie my Soul with Arts, Reasonings and Resignations, then do I expose my self to new temptations and straights: Besides that, I cannot do it without great violence; which leaves me exhausted and dry, so that it behoves me speedily to return to this simple Resignation, knowing that God, in this manner, lets me see, that it is his Will and Pleasure, that a total stop should be put to the operations of my Soul, because he would have all things done by his own divine Activity; and happily he expects no more of me, but this only View in all spiritual Exercises, and in all the pains, temptations and afflictions that may befal me in this life. And the truth is, the quieter I keep my Spirit by this means, the better all things succeed with me; and my crosses and afflictions suddenly vanish. Many times hath my blessed Father St. Frances of Sales, assured me of this.

97. Our late Mother Superiour, encouraged me firmly to persist in that way, and not to fear any thing in this simple View of God: She told me, That that was enough, and that the greater the nakedness, and quietness in God are, the greater sweetness and strength receiveth the Soul, which ought to endeavour to become so pure and simple, that it should have no other support, but in God alone.

98. To this purpose I remember, that a few days since, God communicated to me an Illumination, which made such an impression upon me, as if I had clearly seen him; and this it is, That I should never look upon my self, but walk with eyes shut, leaning on my Beloved, without striving to see nor know the way, by which he guides me, neither fix my thoughts on any thing, nor yet beg Favours of him, but as undone in my self, rest wholly and sincerely on him. Hitherto that Illuminated and Mystical Mistress, whose Words do Credit and Authorize our Doctrine.

SECTION FOURTEEN: *Declaring how the Soul putting it self in the Presence of God, with perfect Resignation, by the pure act of Faith, walks always in virtual and acquired contemplation.*

99. Thou wilt tell me (as many Souls have told me) that though by a perfect Resignation thou hast put thy self in the Presence of God, by means of pure Faith, as hath been already hinted, yet thou doest not merit nor emprove, because thy thoughts are so distracted, that thou canst not be fixed upon God.

100. Be not disconsolate, for thou do'st not lose time, nor merit, neither desist thou from Prayer; because it is not necessary, that during the whole time of recollection, thou should'st actually think on God; it is enough that thou hast been attentive in the beginning; provided thou discontinue not thy purpose, nor revoke the actual attention which thou hadst. As he, who hears Mass, and says the Divine Office, performs his Duty very well, by virtue of that primary actual attention, though afterwards he persevere not, in keeping his thoughts actually fixed on God.

101. This the Angelical Doctor St. Thomas confirms, in the following words (*2.2.quæst.82.art. 13. ad I.*): That first intention only and thinking of God when one Prays, has force and value enough to make the Prayer, during all the rest of the time it continues, to be true, impetratory and meritorious, though all that while there be no actual contemplation on God. See now if the Saint could speak more clearly to our purpose!

102. So that (in the Judgement of that Saint) the Prayer still continues, though the Imagination may ramble upon infinite numbers of thoughts, provided one consent not to it, shift not Place, intermit not the Prayer, nor change the first Intention of being with God. And it is certain, that he changes it not, whil'st he does not leave his Place. Hence it follows in sound

Doctrine, that one may persevere in Prayer, though the Imagination be carried about with various and unvoluntary thoughts. *He prays in Spirit and Truth* (says the Saint in the fore-cited place) *whoever goest to Prayer with the Spirit and Intention of Praying, though afterwards through Misery and Frailty his Thoughts may straggle.* Evagatio vero mentis quæ fit præter propositum, orationis fructum non tollit.

103. But thou'lt say, at least, art thou not to remember when thou art in the presence of God, and often say to him, *Lord abide within me; and I will give my self wholly up to thee?* I answer that there is no necessity for that, seeing thou hast a design to Pray, and for that end went'st to that place. Faith and Intention are sufficient, and these always continue; nay, the more simple that remembrance be, without words, or thoughts, the more pure, spiritual, internal, and worthy of God it is.

104. Would it not be impertinent and disrespectful, if being in the Presence of a King, thou should'st ever now and then say to him, *Sir, I believe Your Majesty is here?* It's the very same thing. By the eye of pure Faith the Soul sees God, believes in him, and is in his Presence, and so when the Soul believes, it has no need to say, *My God thou art here;* but to believe as it does believe, seeing when Prayer-time is come, Faith and Intention guide and conduct it to contemplate God by means of pure Faith, and perfect Resignation.

105. So that, so long as thou retractest not that Faith, and Intention of being resigned, thou walkest always in Faith and Resignation, and consequently in Prayer, and in virtual and acquired Contemplation, although thou perceive it not, remember it not, neither exertest new Acts and Reflections thereon; after the example of a Christian, a Wife, and a Monk; who, though they exert us new Acts and Remembrances, the one as to his Profession, saying, *I am a Monk*, the other as to her Matrimony, saying *I am a Wife*, and the third as to his Baptism, saying, *I am a Christian*, they cease not for all that from being, the one Baptized, the other Married, and the third Professed. The Christian shall only be obliged to do good Works in Confirmation of his Faith; and to believe more with the Heart, than with the Mouth: The Wife ought to give demonstrations of the Fidelity which she promised to her Husband: And the Monk of the Obedience which he made profession of to his Superiour.

106. In the same manner, the inward Soul being once resolved to Believe, that God is in it, and that it will not desire nor act any thing but through God, ought to rest satisfied in that Faith and intention, in all its Works and Exercises, without forming or repeating new Acts of the same Faith, nor of such a Resignation.

SECTION FIFTEEN: *A Sequel to the Same Matter*

107. This true Doctrine serves not only for the time of Prayer, but also after it is over, by Night and by Day, at all Hours, and in all the daily Functions of thy Calling, thy duty and Condition. And if thou tell me, that many times thou forgettest during a whole day, to renew thy resignation, I answer, that though it seem to thee, that thou are diverted from it, by attending the daily occupations of thy Vocation, as Studying, Reading, Preaching, Eating, Drinking, doing Business, and the like; thou art mistaken; for the one destroys not the other, nor by so doing doest thou neglect to do the Will of God, nor to proceed in virtual Prayer, as St. Thomas says.

108. Because these occupations are not contrary to his Will, nor contrary to thy Resignation, it being certain, that God would have thee to Eat, Study, take Pains, do Business, &c. So that to perform these Exercises, which are conform'd to his Will and Pleasure, thou departest not out of his Presence, nor from thine own Resignation.

109. But if in Prayer, or out of it thou should'st willingly be diverted or distracted, suffering thy self deliberately to be transported into any Passion; then it will be good for thee to revert to God, and return into his Divine Presence, renewing the purest of Faith and Resignation. However it is not necessary to exert those Acts, when thou findest thy self in dryness, because dryness is good and holy, and cannot, how severe soever it be, take from thy Soul the Divine Presence, which is established in Faith. Thou oughtest never to call dryness distraction, because in beginners it is want of sensibility, and in proficient abstractedness, by means whereof, if thou bear it out with constancy, resting quiet in thine own emptiness, thy Soul will become more and more inward; and the Lord will work wonders in it.

110. Strive then when thou comest from Prayer, to the end thou mayst return to it again, not to be distracted, nor diverted; but to carry thy self with a total resignation to the Divine Will, that God may do with thee and all thine, according to his heavenly pleasure, relying on him as on a kind and loving Father. Never recal that Intention, and though thou beest taken up about the Affairs of the Condition wherein God hath placed thee, yet thou'lt still be in Prayer in the Presence of God, and in perpetual Resignation. Therefore St. John Chrysostom said *(Super, 5. ad Thessolon.)*, *A just man leaves not off to Pray, unless he leaves off to be Just. He always prays, who always does well; the good desire is Prayer, and if the desire be continued, so is also the Prayer.*

111. Thou'lt understand all that has been said, by this clear Example, when a man begins a Journey to *Rome*, every step he makes in the Progress is voluntary, and nevertheless it is not necessary, that at every step he should express his desire, or exert a new act of the Will, saying, *I am going to* Rome, *I go to* Rome: Because, by vertue of that first intention he had of

travelling to *Rome*, the same Will still remains in him; so that he goes on without saying so, though he does not without intending so; you'll clearly find, besides, that this Traveller, with one single and explicit of the Will and Intention, travel, speaks, hears, sees, reasons, eats, drinks, and does several other things, without any interruption to his first intention, not yet of his actual journying to *Rome*.

112. It is just so in the contemplative Soul: A man having once made the resolution of doing the Will of God, and of being in his Presence, he still perseveres in that act, so long as he recals not the same, although he be taken up in hearing, speaking, eating, or in any other external good work or function of his Calling and Quality. St. Thomas Aquinas expresseth all this in few words (*Contra Gentiles; l.3.c.138.Vn 2.*), *Non enim Oportet quod qui propter deum aliquod iter arripuit, in qualibet parte itineris de Deo cogitet actu.*

113. Thou'lt say, that all Christians walk in this Exercise, because all have Faith, and may although they be not internal fulfil this Doctrine especially such as go in the external Way of Meditation and Retiocination. It is true, all Christians have Faith, and more particularly they who Meditate and Consider: But the Faith of those who advance by the inward Way, is much different, because it is a lively Faith, universal and indistinct, and by consequent, more practical, active, effectual, and illuminated; insomuch as the Holy Ghost enlightens the Soul that is best disposed, most, and that Soul is always best disposed, which holds the Mind recollected; so proportionably to the Recollection the Holy Ghost Illuminates. And albeit is be true, that God communicates some light in Meditation, yet it is so scanty and different from that which he communicates to the Mind, recollected in a pure and universal Faith, that the one to the other, is no more than like two or three Drops of Water in respect of an Ocean: since in Meditation two or three particular Truths are communicated to the Soul; but in the internal Recollection, and the Exercise of pure and universal Faith, the Wisdom of God is an abundant Ocean which is communicated in that obscure, simple, general and universal Knowledge.

114. In like manner Resignation is more perfect in these Souls, because it springs from the internal and infused Fortitude, which grows as the internal Exercise of pure Faith, with Silence and Resignation, is continued: In the manner that the Gifts of God's Spirit grow in contemplative Souls; for though these divine Gifts are to be found in all those that are in a State of Grace, nevertheless, they are, as it were, dead, without strength, and in a manner infinitely different from these which reign in contemplative Persons, by reason of their illustration, vivacity and efficacy.

115. From all which, be perswaded, that the inward Soul, accustomed to go daily at certain hours to Prayer, with the Faith and Resignation I have mentioned to thee, walks continually in the Presence of God. All holy, expert and mystical Masters, teach this true and important Doctrine,

because they have all had one and the same Master, who is the Holy Ghost.

SECTION SIXTEEN: *A Way by which one may enter into internal Recollection, through the most Holy Humanity of Lord Christ.*

116. There are two sorts of Spiritual Men Diametrically contrary one to another: The one say, That the Mysteries of the Passion of Christ, are always to be considered and Meditated upon: The others running to the opposite extreme, teach, That the Meditation of the Mysteries of the Life, Passion, and Death of our Saviour, is not Prayer, nor yet a Remembrance of them; but the exalted Elevation to God, whose Divinity Contemplates the Soul in quiet and silence, ought only to be called Prayer.

117. It is certain that our Lord Christ is the Guide, the Door, and the Way; as he himself hath said in his own Words (*John* 14.): I am the way, the truth, and the life. And before the Soul can be fit to enter into the Presence of the Divinity, and be united with it, it is to be washed with the precious Blood of a Redeemer, and adorned with the rich robes of his Passion.

118. Our Lord Christ with his Doctrine and Example, is the Mirror, the Guide of the Soul, the Way and the only door by which we enter into those Pastures of Life Eternal, and into the vast Ocean of the Divinity. Hence it follows, that the Remembrance of the Passion and Death of our Saviour ought not wholly to be blotted out: nay, it is also certain, that whatsoever high elevation of Mind the Soul may be raised to, it ought not in all things to separate from the most holy Humanity. But then it follows, not from hence neither, that the Soul accustomed to internal recollection, that can no longer ratiocinate, should always be meditating on, and considering (as the other Spiritualists say) the most holy Misteries of our Saviour. It is holy and good to Meditate; and would to God that all men of this World practiced it. And the Soul, besides that meditates, reasons and considers with facilitie; ought to be let alone in that state, and not pushed on to another higher, so long as in that of Meditation it finds nourishment and profit.

119. It belongs to God alone, and not to the spiritual Guide, to promote the Soul from Meditation to Contemplation; because, if God through his special Grace, call it not to this state of Prayer, the Guide can do nothing with all his Wisdom and Instructions.

120. To strike a secure means then, and to avoid those two so contrary extreams, of not wholly blotting out the remembrance of the Humanity; and of not having it continually before our eyes; we ought to suppose, that there are two ways of attending to the Holy Humanity; that one may enter at the Divine Port, which is Christ our well being, The first is by considering the Mysteries, and meditating the Actions of the Life, Passion, and Death of our Saviour. The second by thinking on him, by the application of the Intellect, pure Faith, or Memory.

121. When the Soul proceeds in perfecting and interiorizing it self, by means of internal recollection, having for sometime meditated on the Mysteries whereof it hath been already informed; then it retains Faith and Love to the Word Incarnate, being ready for his sake to do whatever he inspires into it, walking according to his Precepts, although they be not alwaies before its Eyes. As if it should be said to a Son, that he ought never to forsake his Father, they intend not thereby to oblige him, to have his Father alwaies in sight, but only to have him alwaies in his Memory, that in time and place, he may be ready to do his Duty.

122. The Soul then that is entered into internal recollection, with the opinion and approbation of an expert Guide, hath no need to enter by the first door of Meditation on the Mysteries, being alwaies taken up in meditating upon them; because that is not to be done without great fatigue to the Intellect, not does it stand in need of such ratiocinations; since these serve only as a means to attain to believing, that which it hath already got the possession of.

123. The most noble, spiritual and proper way for Souls that are Proficients in internal recollection, to enter by the Humanity of Christ our Lord, and entertain a remembrance of him is the second way; eying that Humanity, and the Passion thereof by a simple Act of Faith, loving and reflecting on the same as the Tabernacle of the Divinity, the beginning and end of our Salvation, Jesus Christ having been Born, Suffered, and died a shameful Death for our sakes.

124. This is the way that makes internal Souls profit, and this holy, pious, swift, and instantaneous remembrance of the Humanity, can be no obstacle to them in the course of internal recollection, unless if when the Soul enters into Prayer, it finds it self drawn back; for then it will be better, to continue recollection and mental excess. But not finding it self drawn back, the simple and swift remembrance of the Humanity of the Divine Word, gives no impediment to the highest and most elevated, the most abstracted and transformed Soul.

125. This is the way that Santa Teresa recommends to the contemplative, rejecting the tumultuary Opinions of some School-men. This is the strait and safe way, free from Dangers, which the Lord hath taught to many Souls, for attaining to repose, and the Holy Tranquility of Contemplation.

126. Let the Soul then, when it enters into recollection, place it self at the Gate of Divine Mercy, which is the amiable and sweet remembrance of the Cross and Passion of the Word that was made Man, and Died for Love; let it stand there with Humility, resigned to the Will of God, in whatsoever it pleases the Divine Majesty, to do with it; and if from that holy and sweet remembrance, it soon fall into forgetfulness, there is no necessity of making a new repetition, but to continue silent and quiet in the presence of the

Lord.

127. Wonderfully does St. *Paul* favour this our Doctrine, in the Epistle which he wrote to the *Colossians*, wherein he exhorts them and us, that whether we Eat, Drink, or do anything else, we should do it in the Name, and for the Sake of Jesus Christ. *Omne quod cumq; faritis inverbo, aut in opere, omnia in nomine Jesu Christi facite, gratias agentes Deo & Parti per ipsum.* God grant that we may all begin by Jesus Christ, and that in him, and by him alone, we may arrive at perfection.

SECTION SEVENTEEN: *Of internal and mystical Silence*

128. There are three kinds of silence; the first is of Words, the Second of Desires, and the third of Thoughts. The first is perfect; the second more perfect; and the third more perfect. In the first, that is, of words, Virtue is acquired; in the second, to wit, of Desires, quietness is attained to; in the third of Thoughts, Internal Recollection is gained. By not speaking, not desiring, and not thinking, one arrives at the true and perfect Mystical Silence, wherein God speaks with the Soul, communicates himself to it, and in the Abyss of its own Depth, teaches it the most perfect and exalted Wisdom.

129. He calls and guides it to this inward Solitude, and mystical Silence, when he saies, That he will speak to it alone, in the most secret and hidden part of the Heart. Thou art to keep thy self in this mystical Silence, if thou wouldest hear the sweet and divine Voice. It is not enough for gaining this Treasure, to forsake the World, nor to renounce thine own Desires, and all things created; if thou wean not thy self from all Desires and Thoughts. Rest in this mystical Silence, and open the Door, that so God may communicate himself unto thee, unite with thee, and transform thee into himself.

130. The perfection of the Soul consists not in speaking nor in thinking much on God; but in loving him sufficiently: This love is attained to by means of perfect Resignation and internal Silence, all consists in Works: The love of God has but few Words. Thus St. *John* the Evangelist confirms and inculcates it. (Epist. I. Chap. 3. v. 18) My little Children, let us not love in Word, neither in Tongue, but in Deed and in Truth.

131. Thou art clearly convinced now, that perfect Love consists not in amorous Acts, nor tender Ejaculations, nor yet in the internal Acts, wherein thou tellest God, that thou hast an infinite Love for him, and thou lovest him more than thy self. It may be that at that time thou seekest more thy self, and the love of thy self, than the true Love of God, *Because Love consists in Works, and not in fair Discourses.*

132. That a rational Creature may understand the secret desire and intention of thy Heart, there is a necessity that thou shouldest express it to

him in Words. But God who searches the Hearts, standeth not in need that thou shouldest make profession and assure him of it; nor does he rest satisfied, as the Evangelist says, with Love in Word nor in Tongue, but with that which is true and indeed. What avails it to tell them with great zeal and fervour, that thou tenderly and perfectly loveth him above all things, if at one bitter word, or slight injury, thou doest not resign thy self, nor are mortified for the love of him? A manifest proof that thy love was a love in Tongue and not in Deed.

133. Strive to be resigned in all things with Silence, and in so doing, without saying that thou lovest him, thou wilt attain to the most perfect quiet, effectual and true love. St. *Peter* most affectionately told the Lord, that for his sake he was ready, willingly to lay down his Life; but at the word of a young Damsel, he denied him, and there was an end of his Zeal. *Mary Magdelen* said not a word, and yet the Lord himself taken with her perfect Love, became her Panagyrist, saying that she had loved much. It is internally, then, that with dumb Silence, the most perfect Virtues of Faith, Hope, and Charity are practised, without any necessity of telling God, that thou lovest him, hopest and believest in him; because the Lord knows better than thou do'st, what the internal Motions of thy Heart are.

134. How well was that pure act of Love understood and practised by that profound and great Mistick, the Venerable Gregory Lopez, whose whole Life was a continual Prayer, and a continued Act of Contemplation; and of so pure and spiritual Love of God, that it never gave way to Affections and sensible Sentiments:

135. Having for the space of three Years continued that Ejaculation, *Thy will be done in Time, and in Eternity*; repeating is as often as he breathed; God Almighty discovered to him, that infinite Treasure of the pure and continued Act of Faith and Love, with Silence and Resignation: so that he came to say, That during the thirty six Years he lived after, he alwaies continued in his inward Man; that pure Act of Love, without ever uttering the least Petition, Ejaculation, or any thing that was Sensible, or sprung from Nature. O Incarnate Seraphim, and Dei-fied Man! How well did'st thou know how to dive into that internal and mistical Silence, and to distinguish betwixt the outward and inward Man?

CHAPTER 2

The Spiritual Guide, which Leads the Soul to the Fruition of Inward Peace

Of the Ghostly Father, the Obedience that's due to him; of Indiscreet Zeal, and of Internal and External Penance.

SECTION ONE: *The best way to baffle the Craft of the Enemy, is to be Subjected to a Ghostly Father.*

1. It is every way convenient, to choose a Master experienced in the inward way, because God will not do all, what he did to St. Catharine of Siena, whom he took by the Hand, and immediately taught the mystical Way. If in the Progress of Nature there is a necessity of a Guide; how must it be in the Progress of Grace? If in the outward and visible waies there is need of a Master; how must it be for the internal and secret? If it must be so for the Moral, Scholastic and Exposive, Theology, which are plainly taught; how must it be for that which is mystical, secret, reserved and obscure? If in external and political Actions and Practices it is so; how must it be in the internal Transactions with God.

2. A Guide is in like manner necessary for resisting and overcoming the Craft and Wiles of Satan. St. Austin gave many Reasons why God appointed that in his Church, Doctors and Teachers, men of the same nature with others, should, for Light and Doctrin, have the Precedency: The chief is, to free us from the craft and cunning of the Enemy; for should we be left to our own Dictates and Natural Impulse, for the conduct of our Actions, we would trip and stumble every foot, and at length fall head-long into the Pit; as it happens to Hereticks and proud People: Now if we had

41

had Angels given to us for Masters, then would the Devils have dazled our Eyes by transforming themselves into Angels of Light: therefore it was convenient that for Guides and Counsellors, God should given us men like our selves. And if such a Guide be expert, he'll soon know the tricks and subtilties of the Devil; which being once known, as wanting substance, they soon evanish.

3. A Ghostly Father ought to come from the Hand of God, and therefore without previous Circumspection and Prayer; he is not to be chosen but being once chosen, he is not to be left, but for most urgent reasons; such as are for not knowing the Waies and States, through which God guides the Soul; because no man can teach what he does not know, according to that true Maxim of Philosophy.

4. And if he conceive not (as St. *Paul* saith) the things of the Spirit, that will be Ignorance in him; because they are to be examined Spiritually, and he wants experience: but the spiritual and expert Man sees every thing clearly, and judges of it as it is. If a Guide then wants experience, it is a chief reason why one should leave him, and chuse another more expert; because without such a one, the Soul will not profit.

5. To pass from a bad into a good state, there is no necessity of Counsel; but to change what is good into better, there is need of time, prayer and advice; because every thing which is best in is self, is not best for every one in particular; nor is every thing that is good for one, good for all: *Non omnibus omnia expediunt.* Some are called for the outward and ordinary Way; others for the internal and extraordinary, and all are not in the same state; so that there being so many and various persons who are ingaged in the mystical way, it is impossible for one to make a step in those secret and internal Paths without an experienced Guide, because instead of going right, he'll tumble into a Precipice.

6. When a Soul walks with Fear; doubting if it walk safely, and desires to be clearly rid of these fears and doubtings, the securest way is to submit to a Ghostly Father; because by the internal Light he clearly discovers what is Temptation, and what Inspiration, and distinguishes the motions that spring from Nature, from the Devil, and from the Soul it self, which ought totally to be subjected to him who hath experience, and he can discover the engagements, the Idols and bad habits that hinder the Souls flight; which by this means will not only be delivered from the Snares of the Devil, but will proceed more in one Year, than it could have proceeded in a thousand, with other Guides of no Experience.

7. In the Life of the Illuminated Father, Frier John Tauler, it is related what that Layman who went before him in the State of Perfection, says of himself, How that being taken off from the World, and desirous to be Holy, he gave himself to great abstinence, till at length being extenuated and weak, he fell into a Dream, and heard a voice from Heaven which said to

him, *Man, if thou voluntary kill thy self, before the time, thou shalt pay dear to thy self for it*. Being full of terror, he went into a Desait, and there imparted the way he had taken, and his Abstinence to a holy Anchorite, who, by the favour of Heaven, freed him from that Diabolical Delusion. He told him, That he followed that course of Abstinence that he might please God. But the Anchorite having asked him, By what Advice he did it? And he having made answer By none. The Anchorite replied, That is was a manifest Temptation of the Devil. From that time forward, he opened his Eyes, and knowing his own Perdition, lived alwaies by the Direction of a Spiritual Father; and he himself affirmed, That in seven years space he gave him greater Light, than all printed Books whatsoever could do.

SECTION TWO: *Of the Sequel of the same Matter.*

8. There is far greater advantage to be had from having a Master in the mystical way, then from the use of Spiritual books; because a practical Master tells us in the nick of time, what ought to be done; but in a Book one may fall upon a thing that is less proper, and by that means the necessary Instruction is wanting: Besides, by mystical Books men raise to themselves many false Notions, the Soul thinking to have that, which in reality is hath not, and to be farther on in the mystical State, than as yet it is; whence spring many prejudices and dangers.

9. It is certain that the frequent Reading of mystical Books, which are not founded in practical, but meer speculative Light, does rather hurt than good, because it confounds, instead of, enlightening Souls, and fills them with discursive Notions that might hinder them; since tho' they be Notices of Light, yet they enter from without, render the Faculties dull, and fill them with Ideas instead of emptying them, that God may replenish them with Himself. Many do continually Read in these speculative Books, because they will not submit to him who may tell them, that such Reading is not convenient for them; whereas there is no doubt but if they do submit, and the Guide be a man of Experience, he will not allow it them: And then they would profit, and not mind such Studies as the Souls do who are submitted, have Light, and make improvement. Hence it follows, that it contributes much to inward Quiet and Security, to have an experienced Guide, who may govern and instruct with actual Light, that the Soul may not be deluded by the Devil, nor by its own Judgment and Opinion: However, we do not condemn the Reading of spiritual Books in general, seeing here we speak in particular of Souls purely Internal and Mystical, for whom this Book is written.

10. All holy and mystical Masters confess that the security of a mystical Soul, consists in a cordial Submission to its Ghostly Father, communicating to him, whatever passes within it. And therefore he, who lives after his own

Opinion, without applying himself to a Spiritual Director (tho he take himself to be, and is reputed spiritual) opposes himself to the Doctrine of the Saints, and of enlightened Souls; because the more a Soul is illuminated and united with God, the more humble, submiss, subjected and obedient to the spiritual Guide it ought to be. For proof of this truth, I'll relate what the Lord said to Donna Marina d'Escobar: It is reported in her Life, that being Sick, she asked the Lord, If she should be Silent, and omit the acquainting her spiritual Father with the extraordinary things that happened in her Soul, that she might not tire her self, nor trouble the same Father. To whom the Lord answered, *That not to give an Account of them to her Ghostly Father, would not be well done for three Reasons: First, Because as Gold is tried in the Furnance, and the value of Stones known by touching them with the Touch-stone; so the Soul is purified, and the worth of it known, when the Minister of God tries it by the Touch-stone. Secondly, Because to avoid Errour, it was convenient that matters should be governed, according to the Order instituted by God in his Church, in the Scriptures and in the Doctrine of the Saints. Thirdly, That the Mercies which his Divine Majesty shews to his Servants and pure Souls, may not be concealed, but made manifest, that so Believers may be encouraged to serve their God, and he be glorified in them.*

11. In the same place she hath the following words, conform to the aforesaid truth: My Confessor being Sick, and having enjoyned me that I should not make a full Discovery of all things that happened to me, to him, to whom, in the meantime, I Confessed my self, but only of some with prudence; I bewailed my condition to the Lord, that I had not one to whom I might communicate my affairs; and his Majesty made me answer, Thou hast one already who supplies the want of thy Confessor; tell him all that happens to thee. I presently replied, Not so Lord, Not so Lord. (Why?) said the Lord. Because my Confessor commanded me that I should not give him Account of all; and I ought to obey him. His Majesty said to me, Thou hast pleased me by that answer, and that I might hear thee say so, I said what thou hast heard; do so, yet still thou maist acquaint him with some things, as he himself had thee.

12. What Santa Teresa said of herself, comes in very pat in this place: Whenever (saies she) the Lord commanded me any thing, if my Confessor told me another, I turned to the Lord and told him, that I must obey my Confessor. Afterward his Majesty returned to him, to the end he might enjoyn it me of new. This is sound and true doctrine, which secures Souls, and dissipates the illusions of the Devil.

SECTION THREE: *The Indiscreet Zeal of Souls, and the disordinate Love of our Neighbour, disturb internal Peace.*

13. *There is not a more acceptable Sacrifice to God* (says St. Gregory, In *Ezechiel,1 Hom.12*) *than the ardent Zeal of Soul:* For that Ministry, the Eternal

God sent his own Jesus Christ into the World, and ever since it hath been the most noble and sublime of Offices. But if the Zeal be indiscreet, it brings a notable obstacle to the progress of the Spirit.

14. No sooner does thou find in thy self any new and fervent light, but thou would'st lay thy self wholly out for the good of Souls; and in the mean time, its odds, but that that is self-love, which thou takest to be pure zeal. This uses sometime to put on a garb of a disordinate Desire, of a vain complacency, of an industrious affection and proper esteem; all Enemies to the peace of the Soul.

15. It is never good to love thy Neighbour to the detriment of thine own spiritual good. To please God in purity, ought to be the only scope of thy Works; this ought to be thy only desire and thought; endeavouring to moderate thy disordinate fervour; that tranquillity and internal peace may reign in thy Soul. The true zeal of Souls, which thou oughtest to strive for, should be the true love of thy God. That is the fruitful, efficacious, and true zeal, which doth wonders in Souls, though with dumb Voices.

16. St. *Paul* (I Tim. 4.) recommended to us first the care of our own Souls, before that of our Neighbour. *Take heed unto thy self, and unto thy Doctrine,* said he in his Canonical Epistle. Struggle not to over do, for when it is time convenient, and thou canst be any way useful to thy Neighbour; God will call thee forth, and put thee in the employment that will best suit with thee: That thought belongs only to him, and to thee, to continue in thy rest, disengaged, and wholly resigned up to the Divine will and pleasure. Don't think that in that condition thou art idle: He is busied enough, who is always ready waiting to perform the Will of God. Who takes heed to himself for God's sake, does every thing; because, one pure Act of internal Resignation, is more worth than a hundred thousand Exercises for ones own Will.

17. Though the Cistern be capable to contain much Water, yet it must still be without it, till Heaven favour it with Rain. Be at rest, blessed Soul be quiet, humble and resigned, to every thing that God shall be pleased to do with thee, leave the care to God, for he as a Loving Father, knows best what is convenient for thee; conform thy self totally to his Will, perfection being founded in that, inasmuch as he who doeth the will of the Lord, is (Mat. 12.) his Mothers Son, and Brother of the Son of God himself.

18. Think not that God esteemeth him most, that doeth most. He is most beloved who is most humble, most faithful and resigned, and most correspondent to his own Internal Inspiration, and to the Divine will and pleasure.

SECTION FOUR: *A Sequel to the Same*

19. Let all thy desires be conform to the Will of that God, who can

bring streams of Water out of the dry Rock, who is much displeased with those Souls, which in helping others before the time, defraud themselves, suffering themselves to be transported by indiscreet zeal, and vain complacency.

20. As it was with the Servant of *Elisha*, who (2Kings, c.4.) being sent by the Prophet, that with his Staff he might raise a dead Child; because of the complacency he had, it had not the effect, and he was reproved by *Elisha*. In like manner the Sacrifice of *Cain* was rejected, being the first that was offered to God in the World, through the vain-glory he had of being the first, and more than his own Father *Adam*, in offering Sacrifice to God.

21. In like manner the Disciples of our Lord Christ, were infected with that evil, feeling a vain joy, when they cast out Devils, and therefore were sharply reproved by their Heavenly Master. Before *Paul* Preached to the Gentiles the Gospel of the Kingdom of Heaven, being already a chosen Vessel, a Citizen of Heaven, and chosen of God for that Ministry, it was necessary to try and humble him, shutting him up in close Prison; and wouldst thou become a Preacher without passing through the Tryal of Men and Devils? And couldst thou thrust thy self into so great a Ministry, and produce Fruit, without passing through the fiery tryal of temptation, tribulation, and passive purgation?

22. It concerns thee more to be quiet and resigned in a holy case, than to do many and great things, by thy own judgment and opinion; think not that the heroick Actions which great Saints have done, and do in the Church, are Works of their own Industry; for all things as well spiritual as temporal, to the shaking of the last Leaf, are by Divine Providence Decreed from all Eternity. He that does the Will of God, does all things; this thy Soul ought to endeavour, resting in a perfect Resignation to whatever the Lord is pleased to dispose of thee; acknowledg thy self unworthy of so high a Ministry, as the guiding of Souls to Heaven, and then thou'lt put no obstacle to the rest, internal peace, and heavenly flight of thy Soul.

SECTION FIVE: *Light, Experience, and a Divine Call, are necessary for guiding Souls in the inward Way.*

23. Thou'lt think and with great confidence too, that thou art in a condition, to guide Souls in the way of the Spirit, and perhaps, that may be secret Vanity, spiritual Pride, and plain Blindness; seeing besides, that this high employment requires supernatural Light, total abstraction, and other qualities which I shall mention to thee in the following Chapters; the Grace of a Call is also necessary, without which all is but vanity, confidence and self-conceit; because, tho' it be a holy and good thing to guide Souls, and conduct them to Contemplation; yet how know'st thou that God would have thee so employed? And though thou knowest (which yet is not easie)

that thou hast great Light and Experience, yet what evidence hast thou that the Lord would have thee to be of that Profession?

24. This Ministry is of such importance that it is not our parts to take it upon us, until it please God, by means of our Superiours and spiritual Guides, to place us therein; otherwise it would be a heavy prejudice to us, though it might be profitable to our Neighbour. What availeth it us to gain the whole World to God, if our own Soul thereby suffer detriment?

25. Howsoever evident it may be to thee, that thy Soul is endowed with internal light and experience; the best thing still that thou canst do, is to keep quiet and resigned in thine own nothingness, until God call thee for the Good of Souls: That belongs only to him, who knows thy sufficiency and abstraction: It is not thy part to make that judgment, neither to press into that Ministry; because, if thou are governed by thine own opinion and judgment, in an affair of so high concern, self-love will blind, undo, and deceive thee.

26. If then experience, light, and sufficiency are not sufficient, without the grace of a Call to qualifie one for that employment, how must it be without sufficiency? how must it be without internal light? without due experience, which are gifts not communicated to all Souls; but to abstracted and resigned Souls, and to such as have advanced to perfect annihilation, by the way of terrible tribulation, and passive purgation. Be perswaded, O blessed Soul, that all works, which in this profession are not governed by a true zeal, springing from pure love, and a purged Soul, cloath the Soul with vanity, self-love, and spiritual pride.

27. O how many self confident men by their own judgment and opinion, undertake this Ministry; and instead of pleasing God, emptying and abstracting their own Souls, (though they may do some good to their Neighbour) are filled with Earth, Straw, and Self-conceit! Be quiet and Resigned, renounce thy own Judgment and Desire, sink down into the Abyss of thy own Insufficiency and Nothingness; for there only thou'lt find God, the true Light, thy Happiness, and greatest Perfection.

SECTION SIX: *Instructions and Counsels to Confessors and Spiritual Directors.*

28. The highest and most profitable Ministry, is that of a Confessor, and Spiritual Director; and irreparable are the damages, if it be not well performed.

29. It would be prudently done, to chuse a Patron for so great a Ministry; and that should be the Saints to whom one has greatest Devotion.

30. The chief and most secure Document is, to endeavour the internal and continual retirement; and so he'll walk well in all the exercises and employments of his own State and Calling, particularly in that of the

Confession seat; for when the Soul inwardly Recollected, sallies out to be employed in those external and necessary Exercises, it is God who Illuminates and Works in them.

31. In the Conduct of Souls that are Internal, Documents are not to be given to them, but with mildness and prudence: The Obstacles which hinder the Influences of God, are only to be taken out of the way; however it may be needful to arm them with that holy Counsel of *Sacretum meum mihi*.

32. Many Souls think, that all Confessors are capable of internal Matters; but besides, that is a mistake, it is found by experience to be a great prejudice to communicate them to those who are not so: Because, tho God hath placed them in the inward Way, yet they'll not know these matters, nor advise them to Souls, for want of experience; so that they'll hinder the Progress to Contemplation, enjoying them to Meditate by force, tho' they cannot; and by that means, they stun and ruin instead of helping them in their Flight: for God will have them to advance to Contemplation, and they draw them to Meditation, because they know no other way.

33. If a Confessor would reap Fruit, he is not to look out for any Soul that he may Guide it; it concerns them to come of themselves, and all are not to be admitted, especially if they be Women, because they are not wont to come with sufficient disposition: Not to make ones self a Master, nor be willing to appear so, is an excellent means of doing good.

34. The Confessor is to make use of the name of *Daughter*, as little as he can; because it is most dangerous, God being so Jealous, and the Epithet so Amorous.

35. The Employments which a confessor accepts of, out of his Confession seat, ought to be but few; because God will not have him to be an Agent in Business; and if it were possible, he should not be seen, but in his Confession chair.

36. A God-father, or Executor to a Man's last Will and Testament, he ought not, so much as once, to be, all his life long, because it brings many disturbances to the Soul, all of 'um contrary to the Perfection of so high a Ministry.

37. The Confessor or spiritual Director never ought to Visit his spiritual Daughters, not so much as in case of Sickness, unless he should indeed be then sent for, on the part of her that is ill.

38. If the Confessor procures an inward and outward Recollection, his words will be (tho' he knows it not) like Coals kindled, setting their Souls afire.

39. In the Confessionary, his Reproofs must be ordinarily gentle and sweet, altho' in the Pulpit they are severe and rigorous; because in this he ought to be raging as a Lyon, and in that, he ought to put on the meekness of a Lamb: O how powerful is sweet Reproof for Penitents! In the Confessionary they are already moved; but in the Pulpit their blindness and

hardness, makes it necessary to frighten 'um: yet these ought to be perswaded and reproved rigorously, who come indisposed, and would have Absolution by force.

40. When all that is possible, is done for the benefit of Souls, the Fruit of it is not to be lookt after; because the Devil doth subtilly make that seem his own, which is God's; and assaults with self Conceit and vain Complacency, the capital Enemies of Annihilation; which the Confessor always ought to bring about for such a spiritual Dying.

41. Altho' he often see that Souls are not advantaged, and that those which are edified, loose the Spirit, let him not be disquieted at this, but possess himself in peace, like the Guardian Angles; then let him take courage inwardly, with the sense of his own Sincerity, because sometimes God suffers such a thing among other ends, to humble him.

42. The Confessor ought to avoid himself, and perswade the Souls under his conduct, also, to avoid all sort of outwardness, because it is much abhorred by the Lord.

43. Although he ought not to order Souls to be Communicated, nor take any Communion from 'em, whether for Tryal or Mortification (since there are infinite waies of Trying 'em and Mortifying 'em, without so great a prejudice) yet he ought not to be niggardly with those Souls which are moved by a true Desire, because Jesus Christ indured not to be shut up.

44. Experience shews us that 'tis a difficult thing to fulfil a Penance, when it is great and immoderate: 'tis alwaies best to have it, of some profitable and moderate matter.

45. If the Spiritual Father shews, with any singularity, a greater affection to a Daughter, and such as gives very great disturbance to others of her Sex: here he must use privacy and prudence, and must not speak to any with particularity; because the Devil loves to make strife with the Guide of Souls, and makes use of those very words to disturb others.

46. The continual and principle Exercise of Souls, purely Mystical, must be in the interior Man, producing with privacy, the destruction of Self-love, and the encouraging of 'em to the enduring of inward Mortifications; by which the Lord Cleanses, Annihilates and perfects them.

47. The Desire of Revelations, uses to be a great hindrance to the interior Soul, especially to Women; and there is not an ordinary Dream, but they will Christen it with the name of a Vision. 'Tis necessary to shew abhorrence to all these hindrances.

48. Although Silence be a difficult thing to Women, in the things which the Director orders 'em, yet must he procure it: since it is not good that the things inspired into him from the Lord, should become the Mark for Censures to shoot at.

SECTION SEVEN: *Wherein the same thing is treated of; Discoursing the*

Interests which some Confessors and Spiritual Directors use to have; in which are declared the Qualities which they ought to have for the Exercise of Confession, and also for the Guiding of Souls through the Mystical Way.

49. The Confessor ought to get Penitents incouraged to Prayer; especially when they often present themselves at his Feet, and make known to him their Desire that they have of their Spiritual Good.

50. The Maxim which the Confessor ought mostly to observe, that he may never come into Perdition, is, Not to accept any Present, though the whole World were offered him.

51. Though there are abundance of Confessors, yet they are not all good ones, because some of 'em know but little; others are very Ignorant; others betake themselves to the Applauses of the Gentry; some seek the Favours of their Penitents; some their Presents; some are full of Spiritual Ambition, and seek Credit and Fame, getting a multitude of Spiritual Children to themselves; others affect their Mastership and Command; other, affect the Visions and Revelations of their Spiritual Children, and instead of despising 'em, the only way of securing 'em to Humility, they commend 'em, that they may not leave 'em off and make them write 'em that they may shew'em abroad for Ostentation: All this is Self-love and Vanity in these Guides, and great prejudice to the Spiritual Profit of Souls: since it is certain, that all these respects and interests serve only to hinder the use and exercise of their Office, with advantage and profit; which requires an universal freedom from such things, and whose end and aim ought only to be the glory of God.

52. Other Confessors there are, which with ease and lightness of Aeart, do believe, and approve, and commend all Spirits: Others falling into the vicious extream, do condemn without any reserve, all Visions and Revelations; such things are neither to be believed all, nor condemned all: Others also there are who are so enamoured of the Spirit of their Spiritual Daughters, that whatever they Dream, let 'em be never so much Deceit, they reverence 'em as sacred Mysteries! O what a world of Miseries are known in the Church by these means! Others Confessors there are also, having on the Garb of worldly Courtesie and Civility, having little regard to the holy Place of the Confessionary, discoursing with their Penitents concerning things vain, superfluous distractive, and far from that decency which the Sacrament requires, and from that disposition which should be fit to receive divine Grace; making particularly like discourses, and about the Houshold Affairs of their Penitents, before they come to accuse themselves of their sins: whereupon that little Devotion which they brought along with 'em to the Sacrament, becomes cool'd and good for nothing: Sometimes it happens that many Penitents are fain to wait to be Confessed, who are full of business of their own, and when they see such a long demur, they grow

weary and sad, and fall into impatience, losing the actual disposition of Mind wherewith they were before prepared to receive so healthful a Sacrament: whereupon the medley of these distractive, superfluous and vain matters, not only make 'em lose their precious time, but also prejudiceth the holy Place, the Sacrament; the disposition of the Penitent who is confessed, and that of others who wait to be confessed; all of 'em considerable mischiefs, and worthy to be redressed.

53. For Confession, there are some good; but for the Government of Spirits by the mystical Way, there are so few (says Father John Davila) that in a thousand, you shall possibly find one: St. Francis of Sales says, *One among ten thousand*: And the illuminated Thauler says, *That in a hundred thousand, it was a hard thing to find one expert Master of Spirit*. The reason is, because there are so few who dispose themselves to receive the mystical Science: *Pauci ad eam recipiendam se disponunt*; said Henry Arpias (*Lib. 3. Par. 3. Cap. 22*) Would to God it were not so true as it is. For then there would not be so many Cheats in the World, and there would be more Saints and fewer Sinners.

54. When the spiritual Guide desires effectually, that all should be in love with Vertue, and the love which they have of God, is pure and perfect, with few Words, and few Reasons, he will reap a very great deal of Benefit.

55. If the interiour Soul, when it is in the cleansing it self of Passions, and in the time of abstraction, has not a sure Guide to curb in the retirement and solitude, to which its Inclination and great Propension draws it, it will be unable and unfit for exercises of Confession, Preaching and Study, and also for those of its own Obligation, State and Calling.

56. The skilful Director therefore, ought to mind carefully when the Powers of it begin to be imployed in God, that there may not be given too free access to solitude, commanding the Soul not to omit the outward exercises of its state, as of Study, and other Employments, altho' they should seem distractive, so that they be not contrary to his Calling; because the Soul is so much Abstracted in Solitude, is so turned inward in its retirement, and is removed to such a degree from Exteriority, that if it afterwards apply it self again, it doth it with toyl and resistance, and with prejudice to its powers, and the strength and soundness of Head: which is considerable hurt, and worthy the weighting of spiritual Directors.

57. But if these have no Experience, they will not know when the abstraction is formed, and at the same time, thinking it Holy Counsel, will encourage 'em to Retirement, and find destruction in it: O how necessary it is that the Guide be expert in the spiritual and mystical way!

SECTION EIGHT: *Pursues the same Matter*

58. Those that govern Souls without Experience go in the dark, and arrive

not at the Understanding of the states of the Soul in their internal and supernatural Operations, they only know that sometimes the Soul is well, and that it has Light; other times that it is in Darkness; but what the state of all these is, and what is the Root from whence these Changes grow, they neither know nor understand, nor can verifie it by means of Books, till they come to find it experimentally in themselves, in whose Furnace the true and actual Light is made.

52. If the Guide hath not passed himself thro' the secret and painful ways of the interiour walk, how can he comprehend or approve it? It will be no small favour to the Soul, to find one only experienced Guide to strengthen it in insuperable Difficulties, and assure it in the continual doubts of this Voyage: otherwise he will never get to the holy and precious Mount of Perfection, without an extraordinary and singular Grace.

60. The spiritual Director, which lives disinterested, longs more for the internal Solitude than the Employment of Souls: and if any spiritual Master is displeased when a Soul goes from him, and leaves him for another Guide, 'tis a clear sign, that he did not live disinterested, nor sought purely the Glory of God, but his own proper Esteem.

61. The same loss and evil comes, when the Director is secretly diligent to draw some Soul to his direction, which goes under the government of another Guide; this is a notable mischief; for if he holds himself for a better Director than t'other, he is proud; and if he knows himself to be a worse, he is a Traytor to God, to that Soul, and to himself, during the prejudice he does to the advantage and good of his Neighbours.

62. In like manner there is another considerable hurt that discovers it self in spiritual Masters, which is, that they do not suffer the Souls Guided by 'em, to communicate with others, tho they are more Holy, Learned, and Expert than themselves: all this is Interest, Self-love, and Esteem of themselves. They do not permit Souls thus to unburthen and vent themselves, for fear they should loose 'em, and that it may not be said, that their Spiritual Children seek that Satisfaction in others, which they cannot find in them; and for the most part, by these imperfect ends, they hinder Souls from being advantaged.

63. From all these, and infinite other imputations, the Director is free that is once arrived at hearing the inward Voice of God, by having passed through Tribulation, Temptation, and passive Purgation; because that interior Voice of God works innumerable and marvelous Effects in the Soul, which gives place to it, hearkens to it, and relishes it.

64. It is of so great Efficacy, that it rejects worldly Honour, Self-conceit, Spiritual Ambition, the desire of Fame, a wish to be Great, a presumption of being the only Man, and thinking that he knows all things; it bids adieu to Friends, Friendship, Visits, Letters of Complement, Commerce of the Creature, Interest with Spiritual Children, Mastership, and Business; it turns

away too much inclination to Confessor-ship, the Affection that is disorder'd in the Government of Souls, that makes a man think he is fitting for it; it moves Self-love, Authority, Presumption, treating of Profit, making a shew of the Letters which a man writes, shewing those writ by his Spiritual children, to make known what a great Workman he is; it turns away the Envy of other Masters and Teachers, and the procuring more Customers to his chair of Confession.

65. Lastly, this interiors Voice of God in the Soul of Director, begets a mean Value, and Solitariness, and Silence, and Forgetfulness of Friends, Relations and Spiritual Children; because it makes him never remember 'em, but when they are speaking to him. This is the only sign to know the Disinterestedness of a Master; and therefore such a one doth more good by silent, than thousands of others that make never so great a noise with their infinite Documents.

SECTION NINE: *Shewing how a simple and ready Obedience is the only means of for walking, safely in the inward Way, and of procuring internal Peace.*

66. If thou dost in good earnest resolve to deny thy Will, and do God's Obedience is the necessary means; whether it be by the indissoluble knot of thy Vow, made in the hands of thy Superior in thy Religion, or the free tying of thy self by the Dedication of thy Will, to a Spiritual and expert Guide, that hath the Qualities sewn before in the precedent Chapters.

67. Thou wilt never get up the Mountain of Perfection, nor to any high Throne of Peace Internal, if thou art only govern'd by thy own Will: This cruel and fierce Enemy of God, and of thy Soul, must be conquered; thy own Direction, thy own Judgement, must be subdued and deposed as Rebels, and reduced to Ashes by the Fire of Obedience: there it will be found, as in a Touch-stone, whether the Love thou followest be thine own, or Divine; there in that Holocaust must thine own Judgment, and thine own Will be Annihilated and brought to its last Substance.

68. An ordinary Life under Obedience, is worth more than that which of its own will doth great Pennance; because obedience and subjection, besides that they are free from the deceits of Satan, are the truest Holocaust which can be sacrificed to God on the Altar of our Heart. Which made a great Servant of God say, *That he had rather gather Dung by Obedience, than be caught up to the third Heaven of his own will.*

69. You will know that Obedience is a ready way to arrive quickly at Perfection: 'tis impossible for a Soul to purchase it self true peace of Heart, if it doth not deny and overcome its own judgment and rebellion: And the means of denying and overcoming ones Judgment, is to be willing in every thing to obey with resolution, him that stands in God's place; because the Heart remains free, secure, and unburthen'd by all that which goes from the

Mouth, with true Submission, to the Ears of the Spiritual Father. (*Effundite coram illo corda vestra*, Pl. 61.) The most effectual means therefore to advance in the way of the Spirit, is to imprint this in the Heart, that a man's spiritual Director stands in God's place, and whatever he orders and says, is said and ordered from the Divine Mouth.

70. The Lord often-times manifested to that venerable Mother Ann Mary of S. Joseph a *Fransciscan* Nun; That she should rather obey her spiritual Father, then Himself, *(History of her Life, § 42.)* To the venerable Sister Catherine Paulucci, the Lord also one day said, *You ought to go to your spiritual Father, with pure and sincere Truth, as if you came to Me, and not inquire whether he be or be not Observant, but you ought to think that he is Governed by the Holy Ghost, and that he is in My stead,* (Her Life, Book 2. Ch. 16) adding, *When Souls shall observe this, I will not permit that any be Deceived by him.* O Divine Words worthy to be imprinted in the Hearts of those Souls which desire to advance in Perfection!

71. God revealed to Lady Marina of Escobar, that if our Lord Christ would have her communicate after his mind, and her spiritual Father should say nay; she was obliged to follow the mind of her spiritual Father: And a Saint was lower'd down from Heaven to tell her the reason of it; which was, *That in the first there might be Cheat, but in the second none.*

72. The Holy Ghost advises us all in the <u>Proverbs (Ch. 3.)</u> that we take Counsel, and trust not in our own Wisom: *Ne innitaris prudentiæ tuæ.* And says by *Tobit*, That, to do well, thou never oughtest to govern thy self with thine own proper judgment; but always must ask others mind and judgment, (<u>Ch. 4. 14.</u> *Consilium semper a sapiente perquire.*) Although the spiritual Father Err in giving counsel, you can never Err in taking it, and following it; because you act wisely: *Qui judiceo alterius operatur, prudenter operatur.* And God doth not suffer Directors to Err, that he may preserve, tho' it should be with Miracles, the visible Tribunal of the spiritual Father; from whence is known with all Safety, what is the Divine Will.

73. Besides, that this is the common Doctrine of all the Saints, of all the Doctors and Masters of Spirit, Christ our Lord gave credit and security to it, when he said, That the spiritual Father should be understood and obeyed just like Himself: *Qui vos audit, mea audit* (<u>St. Luke 10</u>) And this even when their Works do not correspond with their Words and Counsels; as is manifest by <u>St. Matthew, Chap. 1.</u> *Quæcunque dixerint vobis facite, secundum autem opera eorum nolite facere.*

SECTION TEN: *Pursues the Same*

74. The Soul which is observant of holy Obedience, is, as St. Gregory says (*3. Lib. in Job, Cap. 13.*) Possessour of all Vertues: It is rewarded by God for its Humilty and Obedience, illustrating and teaching its own

Guide, to whose direction it ought (as being in God's place) to be every way subject, discovering freely, cleerly, faithfully and simply all the thoughts, all the works, inclinations, inspirations, and temptations that it knows of it self: In this manner the Devil cannot deceive it; and it becomes secure of giving an account of its actions to God without fear, as well those actions which it doth commit, as those it doth omit. Insomuch, that whoever would walk without a Guide, if he is not deceived, he is very near it, because, Temptation will seem Inspiration to him.

75. Thou oughtest to know, that to be perfect, it is not enough to obey and honour Superiors, but it is also necessary to obey and honour Inferiours.

76. Obedience therefore, to make it perfect, must be voluntary, pure, ready, chearful, internal, blind and persevering: Voluntary, without force and fear: Pure, without worldly interest and respect, or self love, but purely for God: Ready, without reply, excuse or delay: Chearful, without inward affliction, and with diligence: Internal, because it must not only be exterior and apparent, but from the mind and heart: Blind, without ones own judgment, but submitting that judgment with the will: to his that Commands it, without searching into the Intention, End, or Reason of the Obedience Persevering, with firmness and constancy unto Death.

77. Obedience (according to St. Bonaventure (*tract. 8. Collationum*) must be ready, without a delay; Devout with tyring, Voluntary without contradiction, Simple, without examination, Persevering without resting; Orderly without breaking off; Pleasant without trouble; Valiant without Faint-heartedness, and Universal without exception. Remember, O blessed Soul! That altho thou hast a mind to do the divine Will, with all diligence, thou wilt never find the way, but by the means of Obedience. When a man is resolved to be governed by himself, he is lost and deceived: Although the Soul have very profound signs, that it is a good Spirit that speaks to it; yet unless it submit to the judgment of the Spiritual Director, let it be esteemed an evil Spirit: So says Gerson, (*Tract. de dist. verar. Num. 19.*) and many other Masters of Spirit.

78. This Doctrine will be confirmed by that case of St. Teresa. The holy Mother, seeing that Lady Catherine of Cordona, led a life of great and rigid Penance in the Wilderness, resolved to imitate her, contrary to the judgment of her spiritual Father, who forbid her; Then the Lord told her (in her Life 366.) You must by no means do this, Daughter; the good way thou hast secure; thou seest all the Penance that *Catherine* doth, but I value more thy Obedience. She from that time forward, vowed to obey her spiritual Father: and in the *26th. Chapter of her Life*, we read, that God often told her, that she must not omit to acquaint her spiritual Father with her whole Soul, and the graces that she had done her, and that she should always take care to obey him in everything.

79. Thou seest how God hath been willing to secure that heavenly and important Doctrine by the holy Scripture, the Saints, the Doctors, by Reasons, and by Examples, a purpose to root out altogether the deceits of the Enemy.

SECTION ELEVEN: *When, and in what things this Obedience doth most concern the interior Soul.*

80. That you may know when Obedience is most necessary, I will advise thee, that when thou shalt find the horrible and importunate suggestions of the Enemy, greatest upon thee, when thou shalt suffer most darkness, anguish, drowth, forsakings, when thou shalt see thy self most beset with temptations, wrath, rage, blasphemy, lust, cursing, tediousness, despair, impatience, and desolation; then 'tis most necessary for thee to believe, and obey an expert Director, resting thy self on his holy Counsel, that thou may'st not suffer thy self to be carried away by the strong perswasion of the Enemy, who would make thee believe in affliction, and heavy desertion, that thou art lost and abhorred by God, that thou art out of his favour, and that Obedience is past doing thee any good.

81. Thou shalt find thy self encompassed with troublesome scruples, griefs, anguish, distress, martyrdoms, distrusts, forsakings of the Creatures, and troubles so bitter, that thy afflictions shall seem past comfort, and thy torments unconquerable. O blessed Soul! how happy wilt thou be, if thou dost but believe thy Guide, and subject thy self to to him and obey him? Then wilt thou walk safe by the secret and interiour way of the dark night, altho thou may'st seem to thy self to live in Errour, and that thou art worse then ever; that thou seest nothing in thy Soul, but abomination and signs of condemnation.

82. Thou wilt think verily, that thou art possessed by an evil Spirit; because the signs of this interior exercise, and horrible tribulation, seem as bad as the invasions of infernal Furies and Devils. Then take care to believe thy Guide firmly, for thy true Happiness consists in thy obedience.

83. You must consider that when the Devil sees a Soul totally denying it self, and submitting to the obedience of its Director, he makes a strange uproar all Hell over to hinder this infinite Good, and this holy Sacrifice: Full of envy and fury as he is, he uses to make strife between the two, inspiring the Soul with wearisomness, anger, aversion, resistance, distrust, and hatred against the Guide, and sometimes he makes use of his Tongue to bespatter him with many Reproaches; But if this Director be an expert one, he laughs at theses subtle Snares and diabolical Craftynesses. And however the Devil may perswade the Souls of such a state, with divers suggestions, not to believe their Director, that they may not obey him, nor

profit under him; yet nevertheless they may believe, and they do believe enough to obey, tho' it be without their own satisfaction.

84. Thou wilt ask of thy Guide some Liberty, or wilt communicate to him some Grace received. If in denying thee that Liberty, or rejecting that Grace, that thou may'st not grow proud, thou withdrawest thy self from his Counsel, and leavest him, it is a sign that the Favour was false, and that thy spirit walks in danger: But if thou doest believe and obey, altho' he do soundly displease thee, 'tis a sign that thou art alive and unmortified; nevertheless, thou wilt profit with that violent and working Medicine: because tho' the inferiour part be troubled and do resent, yet the superiour part of the Soul doth embrace him, and will be humbled and mortified; because it knows that this is the divine Will. And tho' thou dost not know it, yet satisction goes on emproving in thy Soul, and so doth the confidence that thou hast in thy Guide.

85. The means of denying self love, and of laying down ones own judgment, you must know, is subjecting it altogether with true submission to the Counsel of the spiritual Physitian. If he hinders you your pleasure, or demands what you desire not, thousands of false and idle reasons do presently get about his holy Counsel; where it is presently known that the Spirit is not altogether mortified, nor his own judgment blinded, which are irreconcileable Enemies to a ready and blind obedience, and the peace of the Soul.

86. Then 'tis necessary to overcome thy self and thy quick sentiments, to despise those false and lying reasons, by obeying, holding thy tongue, and executing his holy Counsel, because that is the way to root up thy appetite and thine own judgment.

87. For this reason the ancient Fathers, as expert and skilful Masters of Spirit, did exercise their Disciples in divers and extraordinary Ways: To some they gave order to plant Lettice with the leaves downward; to others, to Water dry and whithered Trees; to others, to sew and unsew again, many times, their Cloaths; all marvellous and effectual stratagems to make tryal of simple obedience and to cut by their roots the weeds of their own Will and Judgment.

SECTION TWELVE: *Treats of the Same*

88. Know that thou canst not fetch one step in the way of the Spirit, till thou endeavourest to conquer this fierce Enemy, thy own judgment: And the Soul that will not know this hurt, can never be cured. A sick man that knows his Disease, knows for certain, that altho' he is adry, yet it is not good for him to drink, and that the Physick prescribed him, tho' it be bitter, yet is profitable for him: Therefore he believes not his Appetite, nor trusts in his own Judgment, but yields himself up to a skilful Physitian, obeying

him in every thing, as the means of his Recovery and Cure: The knowledge that he is sick, helps him not to trust to himself, but to follow the wise judgment of his Doctor.

89. We are all sick of the Disease of self love, and our own judgment; we are all full of our selves; we are alwaies desiring things hurtful to us; and that which does us good, is unpleasant and irksome to us: 'Tis necessary therefore for him that is Sick, to use the means of Recovery; which is, not to believe our own judgments and distemper'd sentiments, but the wise Judgment, of the spiritual and skilful Physitian, without reply or excuse, despising the seeming reasons of self-love; and so, if we obey, we shall certainly recover, and this love of ours, which is the Enemy of our ease, and peace, and perfection, and the spirit, will be overcome.

90. How often will thine own judgment deceive thee? And how much wilt thou change thy judgment with shame, when thou hast trusted to thine own self? If any man should deceive thee twice or thrice, wouldst thou ever trust him more? Why therefore, dost thou repose confidence in thine own judgment, which has so often cozen'd thee? O blessed Soul, believe no more, believe not; subject thy self with true submission and follow blindfold this Obedience.

91. Thou wilt be much satisfied to have an experienced Guide, and wilt esteem him a great Happiness; but 'twil little avail thee, if thou valuest thy own judgment more than his Counsel, and dost not submit to it in all truth and simplicity.

92. Suppose a great man be sick of a dangerous Disease: He has in his House a famous and skilful Physitian; and he quickly knows the Disease, the causes, the conditions, and the state of it, and knowing for certain that the Distemper is to be treated with severe Cauteries he orders *Lenitives* for it: Now, is not this a great disorder? If his sure that *Lenitives* will do little good, and that Cauterizing is the proper way, why does he not apply it to him? Because, altho' the sick person would have his health, yet the Physitian knows best, and that he is not disposed to take those strong Medicines, and therefore like a wise man, orders him gentle *Lenitives*; because tho' he may not presently get up again by 'em , yet he keeps the Disease from being mortal.

93. What matter is it, if you have the best Director in the World, if yet not withstanding you want true submission? altho' he be a man of skill and knows the grievance and the remedy, he doth not apply the proper Physick, which concerns you most to deny your Will; because he knows your very Heart and Spirit, that it is not disposed to let the infirmities of your own judgment be removed. So you will never be cured, and it will be a Miracle, if he can keep you in Grace, with so fierce an Enemy of your Soul about you.

94. Thy Director will scorn all manner of Favours, if he be a wise man; as if thy Spirit may not be well grounded, believe him, obey him, embrace

his Counsel, because with this contempt, if the Spirit be feigned and of the Evil One, the secret Pride formed by him that counterfeits these Spirits, will soon be known; but if the Spirit be real: though thou find'st displeasure in this humiliation: it will serve thee for an extraordinary good.

95. If the Soul take delight in esteem, and in having the favours which it receives from God, made open and publick; if it doth not obey and believes not its Director, which thinks meanly of 'em, 'tis all a lie and cheat, and the Devil is that Angel that transforms himself. The Soul seeing that the skilful Director despises these cheats, if the Spirit be evil, withdraws the feigned affection, which it shewed him, and endeavours by little and little to get from him, seeking some other that its cheats may take with: for the proud can never keep company with those that humble 'em: but on t'otherside, if the Spirit be true and of God, by these means the love and constancy increases by enduring 'em, desiring much more its own contempt, from whence the soundness and sincerity of the Spirit becomes qualified without deceit.

SECTION THIRTEEN: *Frequent Communion is an effectunl means of getting all Vertues, and in particular, Internal Peace.*

96. There are four things the most necessary to get Perfection and internal Peace: The first is Prayer, the second Obedience; the third frequent Communion; the fourth internal Mortification. And now since we have treated of Prayer and Obedience, it will be fitting to treat also of Communion.

97. You ought to know that many Souls there are that deprive themselves of the infinite benefit of this precious Food, by judging that they are not sufficiently prepared, and that no less than an Angelical Purity is necessary for it. if thou hast a pure end, a true desire of doing the Will of God, without looking at sensible Devotion, or thine own Satisfaction, come with confidence, because thou art well disposed.

98. On this Rock of Desiring to do the Divine will, all difficulties must be broken, all scruples overcome, all temptations, doubts, fears, resistances and contradictions: And although the best Preparation for the Soul, be often Communicating, because one Communion disposes it for another; yet I will shew the two ways of Preparation: The first for the exteriour Souls which have good Desire and Will. And the second, for Spiritual Ones which live Internally, and have a greater Light and Knowledge of God, of his Mysteries, of his Operations and Sacraments.

99. The Preparation for the exterior Souls, is to be Confessed and retire from the Creatures, before the Communion to stand still and consider whet is to be received, and who is it that receives it, and that he goes to do the greatest business in the World, which is to receive the great God. What a

singular favour is that Purity it self condescends to be received by Faith! Majesty by Vileness! the Creatour by the Creature!

100. The second Preparation in order to the interiour and spiritual Souls, must be to endeavour to live with greater Purity and Self-denial, with an universal taking ones self off from the World, with an inward Mortification and continual Retirement: and when they walk in this Way, they have no need of any actual preparation, because their Life is a continual and perfect Preparation.

101. If thou do'st not know these Vertues in thy Soul, for the same reason thou must often draw near to this Sovereign Table to get 'em. Never let it hinder thee, to see thy self dry, defective and cold; because frequent Communion is the Physick that cures those diseases, and increases Vertue: for the same reason that thou art Sick, thou must go to the Physian; and that thou art Cold to the Fire.

102. If thou drawest near with humility, with a desire of doing the Divine Will, and with the leave of thy Confessor, thou mayst receive it every day, and every day thou wilt grow better and better. Never be afraid for seeing thy self without that affectionate and sensible love, which some men say is necessary: because this sensible affection is not perfect, and ordinarily it is given to weak and nice Souls.

103. Thou wilt say that thou feelest thy self indisposed, without devotion, without fervour, without the desire of this Divine food, so as to ask how thou must frequent it? believe for certain, that none of these things doth hinder or hurt thee, whilst you preserve this purpose firm, not to sin, and your Will determined to avoid every offence: and if thou hast confessed all those that thou couldst remember, doubt not but that thou are well prepared to come to this Heavenly and Divine Table.

SECTION FOURTEEN: *Pursues the Same Matter*

104. Thou must know that in this unspeakable Sacrament, Christ is united with the Soul, is made one thing with it, whose fineness and purity is the most profound and admirable, and the most worthy of consideration and thanks. Great was the pureness of him in being made Man; greater that of dying ignominiously on the Cross for our sake, but the giving of himself whole and entire to man in this admirable Sacrament, admits no comparison: This is singular favour, and infinite pureness: because there is no more to give; no more to receive. O that we could but comprehend him! O that we could but know him.

105. That God being what he is, should be communicated to my Soul! that God should be willing to make a reciprocalty of union with it, which of it self is meer misery! O Souls, if we could but feed our selves at this Heavenly Table! O that we could scorch our selves at this burning fire! O

that we could become one and the same spirit with this Soveraign Lord! who withholds us? who deceives us? who takes us off from burning like *Salamanders*, in the Divine fire of this holy Table?

106. 'Tis true, O Lord, that thou entrest into me a miserable creature, but true also it is, that thou at the same time remainest in thy glory and brightness, and in thy self. Receive me therefore O my Jesus, in thy self, in thy beauty and Majesty. I am infinitely glad that the vileness of my Soul cannot prejudice thy beauty: thou entrest therefore into me, without going out of thy self; thou livest in the midst of thy brightness and magnificence, tho' thou art in my darkness and misery.

107. O my Soul, how great is thy vileness! (*Job 7 Chap.*) how great thy poverty! what is man, Lord, that thou art so mindful of him? that thou visitest him and makest him great? What is man, that thou puttest such an esteem upon him, being willing to have thy delights with him and dwell personally with thy greatnesses in him? how, O Lord, can a miserable creature receive an infinite Majesty? humble thy self, O my soul, to the very depth of nothing, confess thy unworthiness, look upon thy misery, and acknowledge the wonders of the Divine Love, which suffers it self to be mean in this incomprehensible Mystery, that it may be communicated and united with thee.

108. O the greatness of love, which the amiable Jesus is, in a small host? who is there subject in some manner to man, giving himself whole and sacrificing himself for him to the Eternal Father! O Soveraign Lord, keep back my heart strongly, that it may never more return to its imperfect liberty, but all annihilated may die to the world, and remain united with thee.

109. If thou would'st get all Vertues in the highest degree, come blessed Soul, come with frequency to this most holy Table; for there they do all dwell. Eat, O my Soul, of this Heavenly Food, eat and continue, come with humility, come with Faith to feed of this White and Divine Bread: for this is the Mark of Souls, and from hence Love draws its Arrows, saying, Come, O Soul, and eat this savoury Food, if thou would'st get Purity, Charity, Chastity, Light, Strength, Perfection and Peace.

SECTION FIFTEEN: *Declaring when Spiritual and Corporal Penances ought to be used, and how hurtful they are, when they are done indiscreetly according to ones own Judgment and Opinion.*

110. It is to be known, that there are some Souls who, to make too great advances in Holiness, become much behindhand in it, by doing indiscreet Penances; ilke those who would sing more than their strength allows 'em, who strain themselves till they are tired, and instead of doing better, do worse.

111. Many have fallen into this Precipice, for want of subjecting their judgment to their spiritual Fathers; whilst they have imagined, that unless they give themselves up to rigid Penances, they never can be Saints, as if sanctity did only consist in them. They say, that he that sows little, reaps little; but they sow no other seed, with their indiscreet Penances, than Self-love, instead of rooting it up.

112. But the worst of these indiscreet Penances, is, that by the use of these dry and barren Severities, is begotten and naturalized a certain bitterness of heart towards themselves and their neighbours, which is a great stranger to the true Spirit: towards themselves, because they do not feel the sweetness of Christ's Yoke, the sweetness of Charity, but only the asperity of Penances; whereby their nature becomes imbitter'd; and hence it follows, that such men become exasperated with their Neighbours, to the marking and reproving much their faults, and holding of them for very defective, for the same reason that they see 'em go a less rigorous way than themselves: hence they grow proud with their exercises of Penance, seeing few that do after 'em, and thinking themselves better than other folks, whereupon they much fall in the account of their Vertues. Hence comes the envy of others, to see them less penitent and greater favourites of God; a clear proof, that they fixed their confidence in their own proper diligences.

113. Prayer is the nourishment of the Soul; and the Soul of Prayer is internal mortification: for however bodily Penance, and all other exercises chastening the flesh, be good and holy and praiseworthy, (so as they be moderated by discretion, according to the state and quality of every one, and by the help of the spiritual Director's judgment) yet thou will never gain any vertue by these means, but only vanity and the wind of vain-glory, if they do not grow from within. Wherefore now thou shalt know when thou art to use most chiefly External Penances.

114. When the Soul begins to retire from the World and Vice, it ought to tame the body with rigour, that it may be subject to the Spirit and follow the Law of God with ease; then it concerns you to manage the Weapons of Haircloth, Fasting and Discipline, to take from the flesh the roots of sin; but when the Soul enters into the way of the Spirit, imbracing internal mortification, corporal chastisements ought to be relaxed, because there is trouble enough in the Spirit: the heart is weakned, the breast suffers, the brain is weary, the whole Body grieved and disabled for the functions of the Soul.

115. The wise and skillful Directer therefore must consider, not to give way to these Souls to perform such excesses of Corporal and External Penance, to whom he moves the great love of God, which they do conceive in the internal, darksom and cleansing retirement of em; because 'tis not good to spend the Body and the Sprit all at once, nor break their strength by rigorous and excessive Penances, seeing they are weakned by internal

mortification. For which reason St. Ignatius Loyola said very well in his Exercises, That in the cleansing way, Corporal Penances were necessary, which in the illuminating way ought to be moderated, and much more in the unitive.

116. But thou wilt say, That the Saints always used grevious Penances. I answer, that they did 'em not with indiscretion, nor after their own proper judgment, but with the opinion of their Superious and Spiritual Directors which permitted 'em to use them, because they knew them to be moved inwardly by the Lord to those rigours, to confound the misery of sinners by their examples, or for many other reasons. Other times they gave them leave to use them to humble the fervour of their Spirit and counterpoise their Raptures; which are all particular Motives and make not any general Rule for all.

SECTION SIXTEEN: *The great difference between External and Internal Penances.*

117. Know that the Mortifications and Penances which some one undertakes of himself, are light (although they may be the most rigorous, which hithero have been done) in comparison to those he takes from another's hands: because in the first, he himself enters at his own will, which abate the grief, the more voluntary it is, whilst at last he doth but that which he is willing: But in the second, all that is indured, is painful: and the way also painful, in which it is indured, that is to say, by the will of another.

118. This is that which Christ our Lord told St. *Peter*, (St. John 21. 18.) When thou wast young and a beginner in vertue, thou girdest and mortifiedst thy self; but when thou goest to greater Schools, and shall be a proficient in vertue, an other shall gird and mortifie thee: and then if thou wilt follow me perfectly, altogether denying thy self, thou must leave that cross of thine, and take up mine, that is, be contented that another crucifie thee.

119. There must be no difference made between these and those, between thy Father and thy Son, thy Friend and thy Brother; these must be the first to mortifie thee, or to rise up against thee, whether with reason or without reason, thinking the vertue of thy Soul, cheat, hypocrisie or imprudence, and putting stumbling-blocks in the way of thy holy Exercises. This, and much more will befall thee if thou wilt heartily serve the Lord, and make thy self pure from his hand.

120. Hold it for certain, that however good those Mortification and External Penances be, which thou shalt undertake of thine own self, thou wilt never by those only purchase perfection: for although they tame the Body, yet they purifie not the Soul, nor purge the internal Passions, which do really hinder perfect Contemplation and the Divine Union.

121. 'Tis very easie to mortifie the Body by means of the Spirit; but not the Sprit by means of the Body. True it is, that in Internal Mortification, and that of the Spirit, it much concerns you, for conquering your Passions and rooting up your own Judgment and self-love, to labour even to death, without any manner of sparing your self, although the Soul be in the highest state: and therefore the principal diligence ought to be in Internal Mortification: because Corporal and External Mortification is not enough, though it be good and holy.

122. Though a man should receive the punishments of all men together, and do the roughest Penances that ever have been done in God's Church, yet if he do not deny himself and mortifie himself with interiour mortification, he will be far from arriving at perfection.

123. A good proof of this truth is that which befel Saint Henry Suson, to whom after twenty years of rigorous Hair-cloth, Discipline, and Abstinence so great, that even to read 'em is enough to make ones hair stand on end, God communicated light by means of an Extasie, by which he arrived at the knowledge that he had not yet begun, and it was in such a manner, as that, till the Lord mortified him with temptations and great persecutions, he never could arrive at perfection, (his *Life, chap. 23*.) Hence thou wilt clearly know the great difference that there is between External and Internal Penances, and Internal and External Mortification.

SECTION SEVENTEEN: *How the Soul is to carry it self in the Faults it doth commit, that it may not be disquieted thereby, but reap good out of it.*

124. When thou fallest into a fault, in what matter soever it be, do not trouble nor afflict thy self for it: for they are effects of our frail nature, stained by Original Sin; so prone to Evil, that it hath a necessity of a most special Grace and Priviledge, as the most holy Virgin had, to be free and exempt from Venial Sins. (*Council of Trent, Sess. 6. Can. 23*.)

125. If when thou fallest into a fault or a piece of neglect, thou dost disturb and chide thy self, 'tis a manifest sign, that secret pride doth still reign in thy soul: didst thou believe, that thou could'st not more fall into faults and frailties? if God permits some failings even in the most holy and perfect men, it is to leave 'em some remnant of themselves of the time that they were beginners, to keep 'em more secure and humble, it is that they may think always, that they are never departed from that state, whilst they still keep upon the faults of their beginnings.

126. What dost thou marvel at, if thou fallest into some light fault or frailty? humble thy self; know thy misery and thank God that he has preserved thee from infinite sins, into which thou mn't have infallibly fallen, and wouldst have fallen according to thy inclination and appetite: What can be expected from the slippery ground of our nature, but stumps, bryers and

thorns? 'Tis a Miracle of Divine Grace, not to fall every moment into faults innumerable. We should offend all the World, if God should not hold his hand continually over us.

127. The common enemy will make thee believe, that, as soon as thou fallest into any fault, thou dost not go well grounded in the way of the Spirit, that thou walkest in Error, that thou hast not in earnest reformed thy self, that thou didst not make well the general confession, that thou hast not true grief, and therefore art out of God and of his favour: and if thou shalt sometimes commit again, by misfortune, a venial fault, how many fears, frights, confusions, discouragements and various discourses will the Devil put into thy herrt? he will represent to thee, that thou employest thy time in vain; that thou dost just as much as comes to nothing; that thy Prayer doth thee no good; that thou disposest not the self, as thou oughtest, to receive the holy Sacrament; that thou dost not mortifie thy self, as thou promiseth to God daily; that Prayer and Communion without Mortification is meer vanity: herewith would he make thee distrust of the Divine Grace, telling thee of thy misery and making a Gyant of it, and putting into thy head, that every day thy Soul grows worse instead of better, whilst it so often repeats those failings.

128. O blessed Soul, open thine eyes, suffer not thy self to be carried away by the deceitful and gilded tricks of Satan, who seeks thy ruine and cowardise with these lying and seeming reasons: Cut off these discourses and considerations, and shut the gate against these vain Thoughts and diabolical Suggestions; lay aside these vain fears, and remove this faint-heartedness, knowing thy misery, and trusting in the Mercy Divine: and if to morrow thou dost fall again, as thou did'st to day, trust again the more in that supream, and more than infinite Goodness, so ready to forget our faults, and receive us into his Arms as dear Children.

SECTION EIGHTEEN: *Treateth of the same Point*

129. At all times therefore thou oughtest, when thou seest thy self in fault, with out losing time, or making discourses upon the failing, to drive away vain Fear and Cowardise, without disturbing or chiding thy self, but knowing thy fault with Humility, looking on thy misery, rowling thy self with a loving confidence on the Lord, going into his presence, asking him Pardon heartily, and without noise of words; keep thy self reposed in doing this, without discoursing whether he hath or hath not forgiven thee, returning to thy Exercises and Retirements, as if thou has'st not Sinned.

130. Would not he be a meer Fool, which running at Turneament with others, and falling in the best of the Career, should lie weeping on the ground, and afflicting himself with discourses upon his fall? Man (they would tell him) loose no time, get up and take the Course again; for he that

rises again quickly, and continues his Race, is as if he had never fallen.

131. If thou hast a desire to get to a high degree of Perfection and inward Peace, thou must use the Weapon of Confidence in the Divine Goodness, night and day, and always when thou fallest. This humble and loving Conversation, and total Confidence in the Mercy Divine, thou must exercise in all faults, imperfections, and failings that thou shalt commit, either by advertence or inadvertency.

132. And although thou often fallest, and seest thy Pusillanimity, and endeavour to get courage, and afflict not thy self; because what God doth not do in forty Years, he sometimes doth in an instant, with a particular Mystery, that we may live low and humble, and know that 'tis the Work of his powerful Hand, to free us from Sins.

133. God also is willing, of ineffable Wisdom, that, not only by Vertues, but also by Vices and the Passions wherewith the Devil seeks and pretends to strike us down to the bottomless Pit, we make a Ladder to scale Heaven with. *Ascendamus etiam per vitia & passiones nostras*, says St. Austine (*Serm. 3. de Ascens.*) That we may not make Poison of Physick, and Vices of Vertues, by becoming vain by 'em; God would have us make Vertues of Vices, healing us by that very thing which would hurt us: So says St. Gregory, *Quia ergo nos de medicamento vulnus facimus, facit ille de vulnere medicamentum; ut qui virtute percutimur, vitio curemur,* (*Lib. 37.c.9.*)

134. By means of small failings, the Lord makes us know that his Majesty is that which frees us from great ones; and herewith he keeps us humbled and vigilant; of which our proud Nature hath most need: And therefore though thou oughtest to walk with great care, not to fall into any fault or imperfection, if thou seest thy self fallen once and a thousand times, thou oughtest to make use of the Remedy which I have given thee, that is, a loving Confidence in the Divine Mercy: These are the Weapons with which thou must fight and conquer Cowardise and vain Thoughts: This is the means thou oughtest to use, not to lose time, not to disturb thy self, and reap good: This is the Treasure wherewith thou must enrich thy Soul: and lastly, hereby must thou get up the high Mountain of Perfection, Tranquility and Internal Peace.

CHAPTER 3

The Spiritual Guide, which Brings the Soul to the getting of Inward Peace

Of Spiritual Martyrdoms whereby God Purges Souls; of Contemplation, infused and passive; of Perfect Resignation, Inward Humility, Divine Wisdom, True Annihilation, and Internal Peace.

SECTION ONE: *The Difference between the Outward and Inward Man.*

1. THERE are two sorts of Spiritual Persons, Internal and External: these seek God by without, by Discourse, by Imagination and Consideration: they endeavour mainly to get Vertues, many Abstinences, Maceration of Body, and Mortification of the Senses: they give themselves to rigorous Penance; they put on Sack-cloth, chastise the flesh by Discipline, endeavour silence, bear the presence of God, forming him present to themselves in their Idea of him, or their Imagination, sometimes as a Pastor, sometimes as a Physician, and sometimes as a Father and Lord: they delight to be continually speaking of God, very often making fervent Acts of Love; and all this is Art and Meditation: by this way they desire to be great, and by the power of voluntary and exteriour Mortifications, they go in quest of sensible Affections and warm Sentiments, thinking that God resides only in them, when they have 'em. This is the External Way, and the Way of Beginners, and though it be good, yet there is no arriving at Perfection by it; nay, there is not so much as one step towards it, as Experience shews in many, that after fifty years of this external exercise, are

void of God, and full of themselves, having nothing of spiritual Men, but just the name of such.

2. There are others truly Spiritual, which have passed by the beginnings of the Interiour Way which leads to Perfection and Union with God; and to which the Lord called 'em by his infinite Mercy, from that outward Way, in which before they exercised themselves. These men retired in the inward part of their Souls, with true Resignation into the Hands of God, with a total putting off and forgetting even of themselves; do always go with a rais'd Spirit to the Presence of the Lord, by the means of pure Faith, without Image, Form or Figure, but with great assurance founded in tranquility and rest Internal: in whose infused meeting and entertainment, the spirit draws with so much force, that it makes the Soul contract inwardly, the Heart, the Body and all the Powers of it.

3. These Souls, as they are already passed by the interiour Mortification, and have been cleansed by God with the Fire of Tribulation, with infinite and horrible Torments, all of them ordained by his hand, and after his way, are Masters of themselves, because they are intirely subdued and denied; which makes them live with great Repose and internal Peace: and although in many occasions they feel Resistance and Temptations, yet they become presently Victorious, because being already Souls of Proof, and indued with Divine Strength, the motions of Passions cannot last long upon them; and although vehement Temptations and troublesome Suggestions of the Enemy may persevere a long time about them, yet they are all conquer'd with infinite gain; God being he that Fights within them.

4. These Souls have already procured themselves a great Light, and a true Knowledge of Christ our Lord, both of his Divinity and his Humanity: They exercise this infused Knowledge with a quiet Silence in the inward entertainment, and the superiour part of their Souls, with a Spirit free from Images and external Representations, with a love that is pure and stripped of all Creatures; they are raised also from outward Actions to the love of Humanity and Divinity; so much as they enjoy, they forget, and in all of it they find that they love their God with all their Heart and Spirit.

5. These blessed and sublimated Souls take no pleasure in any thing of the World, but contempt and in being alone, and in being forsaken and forgotten by every body: They live so disinterested and taken off, that though they continually receive many supernatural Graces, yet they are not changed, no not at those inclinations, being just as if they had not received 'em, keeping always in the in-most of their Hearts a great lowliness and contempt of themselves; always humbled in the depth of their own unworthiness and vileness: In the same manner they are always quiet, serene, and possessed with evenness of mind in Graces and Favours extraordinary, as also in the most rigorous and bitter Torments. There is no News that chears 'em; no Success that makes them sad; Tribulation never

disturb them; nor the interiour, continual and divine Communication make 'em vain and conceited; they remain always full of holy and filial Fear, in a wonderful Peace, Constancy and Serenity.

SECTION TWO: *Pursues the Same*

6. In the external Way they take care to do continual Acts of all the Vertues, one after another, to get to the attainment of 'em: They pretend to purge Imperfections with Industries, proportionable to Destruction; they take care to root up Interests, one after another, with a different and contrary Exercise. But though they endeavour never so much, they arrive at nothing: because we cannot do any thing which is not Imperfection and Misery.

7. But in the inward Way and loving Entertainment in the Presence Divine, as the Lord is he that works, Vertue is established, Interests are rooted up, Imperfections are destroy'd and Passions removed; which makes the Soul free unexpectedly, and taken off, when occasions are represented, without so much as thinking of the good which God of his infinite Mercy prepared for 'em.

8. It must be known that these Souls, though thus Perfect, as they have the true Light of God, yet by it they know profoundly, their own miseries, weakness and imperfections, and what they yet want to arrive at Perfection, towards which they are walking; they are afflicted and abhor themselves; they exercise themselves in a loving fear of God, and contempt of themselves, but with a true Hope in God, and Dis-confidence in themselves. The more they are humbled with true contempt and knowledge of themselves, the more they please God, and arrive at a singular respect and veneration in his Presence. Of all the good Works that they do, and of all that they continually suffer, as well within as without, they make no manner of account before that Divine Presence.

9. Their continual Exercise is, to enter into themselves, in God, with quiet and silence; because there is his Center, Habitation and Delight. They make a greater account of this interiour Retirement, than of speaking of God; they retire into that interiour and secret Center of the Soul, to know God and receive his Divine Influence, with fear and loving reverence; if they go out, they go out only to know and despise themselves.

10. But know that few are the Souls which arrive at this happy State; because few there are that are willing to embrace contempt, and suffer themselves to be Refined and Purified; upon which account, although there are many that enter into this interiour Way, yet 'tis a rare thing for a Soul to go on, and not stick upon the entrance. The Lord said to a Soul, "This inward Way is tread by few; 'tis so high a Grace, that none deserves it; few walk in it, because 'tis no other than a Death of the senses; and few there be

that are willing so to Die and be Annihilated; in which disposition this so soveraign a Gift is founded."

11. Herewith thou wilt undeceive thy self, and perfectly know the great difference which there is between the external and internal Way, and how different that Presence of God is which arise from Meditation, from that which is Infused and Supernatural, arising from the interior and infused Intertainment, and from passive Contemplation; and lastly, you will know the great difference which is between the outward and inward Man.

SECTION THREE: *The means of obtaining Peace Internal, is not the Delight of Sense nor Spiritual Consolation, but the denying of Self-love.*

12. It is the saying of S. Bernard, That to serve God, is nothing else but to do Good and suffer Evil. He that would go to Perfection by the means of sweetness and consolation, is mistaken: You must desire no other Consolation from God, than to end your Life for his sake, in the state of true Obedience and Subjection. Christ our Lord's way was not that of Sweetness and Softness, nor did he invite us to any such, either by his words or Example, when he said, --*He that will come after me, let him deny himself, and let him take up his Cross and follow me,* (St. Matth. 24. 26.) The Soul that would be United to Christ, must be conformable to him, following him in the way of suffering.

13. Thou wilt scarce begin to relish the sweetness of Divine Love in Prayer, but the Enemy with his deceitful Craftiness will be kindling in thy Heart desires of the Desert and Solitude, that thou mayest without any bodies hindrance spred the sails to continual & delightful Prayer. Open thine eyes and consider that this counsel and desire is not conformable to the true counsel of Christ our Lord, who has not invited us to follow the sweetness and comfort of our own Will, but the denying of our selves, saying, *Abneget semetipsum*: As if he should say, He that will follow me, and come unto Perfection, let him part with his own Will wholly, and leaving all things, let him intirely submit to the Yoke of Obedience and Subjection, by means of Self-denyal, which is the truest Cross.

14. There are many Souls dedicated to God, which receive from his Hand great Thoughts, Visions, and mental Elevations, and yet for all that, the Lord keeps from 'em, the Grace of working Miracles, understanding hidden Secrets, foretelling future Contingencies, as he communicates these things to other Souls which have constantly gone through Tribulations, Temptations, and the true Cross, in the state of perfect Humility, Obedience and Subjection.

15. O what a great Happiness is it for a Soul to be subdued and subject! what great Riches is it to be Poor! what a mighty honour to be despised! what a height is it to be beaten down! what a comfort is it to be afflicted!

what a credit of knowledge is it to be reputed Ignorant! and finally, what a Happiness of Happinesses is it to be Crucified with Christ! This is that lot which the Apostle gloried in, *Nos autem gloriari oportet in cruce Domini nostri Jesu Christi*) (Gal. 6. 14.) Let others boast in their Riches, Dignities, Delights and Honours; but to us there is no higher honour, than to be denied, despised and crucified with Christ.

16. But what a grief is this, that scarce is there one Soul which despises spiritual pleasures and is willing to be denied for Christ, imbracing his Cross with love, *Multi sunt vocati; pauci vero electi*, (Matt. 22.) says the Holy Ghost: many are they who are call'd to perfection, but few are they that arrive at it: because they are few who imbrace the Cross with patience, constancy, peace and resignation.

17. To deny ones self in all things, to be subject to another's judgment, to mortifie continually all inward passions, to annihilate ones self in all respects, to follow always that which is contrary to ones own will, appetite and judgment, are things that few can do: many are those that teach 'em, but few are they that practise 'em.

18. Many Souls have undertaken, and daily do undertake, this Way; and they perscvere all the while they keep the sweet relish of their primitive Fervour; but this sweetness and sensible delight is scarce done, but presently, upon the overtaking of a Storm of Trouble, Temptation and Dryness (which are necessary things to help a man up the high Mountain of Perfection) they falter and turn back: a clear sign that they sought themselves, and not God or Perfection.

19. May it please God, that the Souls which have had light, and been called to an inward peace, and by not being constant in dryness and tribulation and temptation, have started back may not be cast into outer darkness, with him that had not on him a wedding garment; although he was a servant, for not being disposed, giving himself up to self-love.

20. This Monster must be vanquished, this seven-headed beast of self-love must be beheaded, in order to get up to the top of the high mountain of peace. This Monster put his head every-where; sometimes it gets amongst Relations, which stranglely hinder with their conversation; to which nature easily let's it self be lead; sometimes it gets with a good look of gratitude, into passionate affection, and without restraint, towards the Confessor; sometimes into affection to most subtle Spiritual vain-glories and temporal ones, and niceties of honour; which things stick very close; sometimes it cleaves to spiritual pleasures, staying even in the gifts of God, and in his graces freely bestowed; sometimes it desires exceedingly the preservation of health, and with disguise, to be used well, and its own proper profit, and conveniences; sometimes it would seem well, with very curious subtilties: and lastly, it cleaves with a notable propensity, to its own proper judgment and opinion in all things; the roots of which are closely

fixed in its own will: All these are effects of Self-love, and if they be not denied, impossible it is that a man should ever get up to the height of perfect Contemplation, to the highest, happiess of the loving Union, and the lofty Throne of Peace Internal.

SECTION FOUR: *Of two Spiritual Martyrdoms, wherewith God cleanseth the Soul that he unites with Himself.*

21. Now you shall know that God uses two ways for the Cleansing the Souls which he would perfect and enlighten, to unite 'em closely to himself: The first (of which we will treat in this and the following Chapter) is with the bitter Waters of Afflictions, Anguish, Distress, and inward Torments. The second is, with the burning Fire of an inflamed Love, a Love impatient and hungry: Sometimes he makes use of both in those Souls which he would fill with Perfection; sometimes he puts 'em into the strong steeping of Tribulations, and inward and outward Bitterness, scorching 'em with the Fire of rigorous Temptation; sometimes he puts 'em into the Crucible of anxious and distrustful Love, making 'em fast there with a mighty force; because so much the greater as the Lord would have the Illumination and Union of a Soul to be, so much the more strong is the Torment and the Purgation; because all the Knowledge and Union with God, arises from suffering, which is the truest proof of Love.

22. O that thou would'st understand the great Good of Tribulation! This is that which blots out Sins, cleanses the Soul, and produces Patience: this in Prayer inflames it, inlarges it, and puts it upon the exercise of the most sublime act of Charity: this rejoyces the Soul, brings it near to God, calls it to, and gives it entrance into Heaven: The same is that which tries the true Servants of God, and renders 'em sweet, valiant and constant: that is it which makes God hear 'em with speed. *Ad dominum, cum tribularer, clamavi & exaudivit me*, (Ps. 119.) 'Tis that which Annihilates, Refines and Perfects 'em: and finally, this is that which of Earthly, makes Souls Heavenly, of Humane, Divine, transforming 'em and uniting 'em in an admirable manner with the Lord's Humanity and Divinity. It was well said by St. Augustine, That the Life of the Soul, upon Earth is Temptation. Blessed is the Soul which is always opposed, if it doth constantly resist Temptation. This is the means which the Lord makes use of to Humble it, to Annihilate it, to Spend it, to Mortifie it, to Deny it, to Perfect it, and fill it with this Divine Gifts: By this means of Tribulation and Temptation he comes to Crown and Transform it. Perswade thy self that Temptations and Fightings are necessary for the Soul, to make it Perfect.

23. O blessed Soul, if thou knowest how to be constant and quiet in the Fire of Tribulation, and would'st but let thy self be washed with the bitter Waters of Affliction, how quickly would'st thou find thy self rich in

heavenly Gifts; how soon would the Divine Bounty make a rich Throne in thy Soul, and a goodly Habitation for thee to refresh and solace thy self in it!

24. Know that this Lord hath his repose no where but in quiet Souls, and in those in which the Fire of Tribulation and Temptation hath burnt up the dregs of Passion, and the bitter Water of Afflictions hath washed off the filthy spots of inordinate Appetites; in a word, this Lord reposes not himself any where, but where Quietness reigns, and Self-love is banished.

25. But thou wilt never arrive at this happy State, nor find in thy Soul the precious Pledge of Peace Internal, although thou hast gotten the better of the External Senses by the Grace of God, till it become purified from the disordered Passions of Concupiscence, Self-esteem Desire and Thoughts, how spiritual soever, and many other Interests and secret Vices, which lye within the very Soul of thee, miserably hindring the peaceable entrance of that great Lord into it, who would be united and transformed with thee.

26. The very Vertues acquired, and not purified, are a hindrance to this great Gift of the Peace of the Soul: and more, the Soul is clogged by an inordinate desire of sublime Gifts, by the Appetite of feeling spiritual Consolation, by sticking to Infused and Divine Graces, intertaining it self in 'em, and desiring more of 'em, to enjoy 'em, and finally, by a desire of begin great.

27. O how much is there to be purified in a Soul that must arrive at the holy Mountain of Perfection, and of Transformation with God! O how disposed, naked, denied, annihilated ought the Soul to be, which would not hinder the entrance of this Divine Lord into it, nor his continual Communication.

28. This disposition of preparing the Soul, in its bottom, for Divine Entrance, must of necessity be made by the Divine Wisdom. If a Seraphim is not sufficient to purifie the Soul, how shall a Soul that is frail miserable and without experience, ever be able to purifie it self?

29. Therefore the Lord himself will dispose thee and prepare thee passively by a way thou understandest not, with the Fire of Tribulation and inward Torment, without any other disposition on thy side, than a consent to the internal and external Cross.

30. Thou wilt find within thy self a passive dryness, darkness, anguish, contradictions, continual resistance, inward desertions, horrible desolations, continual and strong suggestions, and vehement temptations of the Enemy; finally, thou wilt see thy self so afflicted, that thou wilt not be able to lift up thy Heart, being full of sorrow and heaviness, nor do the least act of Faith, Hope or Charity.

31. Here thou wilt see thy self forlorn and subject to Passions of impatience, anger, rage, swearing, and disordered appetites, seeming to thy self the most miserable Creature, the greatest Sinner in the World, the most

abhorred of God, deprived and stript of all Vertue, with a pain like that of Hell, seeing thy self afflicted and desolate, to think that thou hast altogether lost God; this will be thy cruel cutting and most bitter torment.

32. But though thou shalt see thy self so oppressed, seeming to thy self to be proud, impatient and wrothful; yet these temptations shall lose their force and power upon thee, they shall have no place in thy Soul, by a secret Vertue, the soveraign Gift of inward Strength, which rules in the in-most part of it, conquering the most affrightening punishment and pain, and the strongest temptation.

33. Keep constant, O blessed Soul, keep constant; for it will not be as thou imaginest, nor art thou at any time nearer to God, than in such cases of desertion; for although the Sun is hid in the Clouds, yet it changes not its place, nor a jot the more loses its brightness. The Lord permits this painful desertion in thy Soul, to purge and polish thee, to cleanse thee and dis-robe thee of thy self; and that thou mayest in this manner be all his, and give thy self wholly up to him, as his infinite Bounty is intirely given to thee, that thou mayest be his delight; for although thou dost groan, and lament, and weep, yet he is joyful and glad in the most secret and hidden place of thy Soul.

SECTION FIVE: *How important and necessary it is, to the interiour Soul, to suffer blindfold this first and Spiritual Martyrdom.*

34. To the end that the Soul of Earthly may become Heavenly, and may come to that greatest good of Union with God, it is necessary for it to be purified in the Fire of Tribulation and Temptation: And although it be true, and a known and approved Maxim, That all those that Serve the Lord, must suffer troubles, persecutions and tribulations: yet the happy Souls which are Guided by God, by the secret way of the interiour Walk, and of purgative Contemplation, must suffer above all, strong and horrible Temptations and Torments, more bitter than those wherewith the Martyrs were crowned in the Primitive Church.

35. The Martyrs, besides the shortness of their Torment, which hardly endured days, were comforted, with a clear light and special help, in hope of the near and sure Rewards. But the desolate Soul that must dye in it self, and put off, and make clean its Heart, seeing it self abandoned by God, surrounded by temptations, darkness, anguish, affliction, sorrows and rigid drowths, doth taste of Death every moment in its painful Torment and tremendous Desolation, without feeling the least comfort, with an affliction so great, that the pain of it seems nothing else but a Death prolonged, and a continual Martyrdom: wherein with great reason it may be said, that although there be many Martyrs, yet there are few Souls which follow Christ our Lord with Peace and Resignation in such Torments.

36. Then it was men that Martyr'd 'em; and God comforted their Souls: but now it is God that afflicts and hides himself; and the Devils, like cruel Executioners, have a thousand ways to torment the Soul and Body, the whole Man being Crucified within and without.

37. Thy sorrows will seem to thee insuperable, and thy afflictions past the power of comfort, and that Heaven rains no more upon thee: thou wilt feel thy self begirt with griefs, and besieged with sorrows Internal, from the darkness of thy powers, from the weakness of discourses: strong Temptations will afflict thee, painful distrusts and troublesome scruples; nay Light and Judgment will forsake thee.

38. All the Creatures will give thee trouble; spiritual Counsels will bring thee pain; the reading of Books, how holy soever, will not comfort thee, as it used to do: If they speak to thee of Patience, they will exceedingly trouble thee: the fear of losing God through thy unthankfulness and want of returns, will torment thee to the Soul; if thou groanest and beggest help of God, thou will find, instead of comfort, inward reproof and dis-favour; like another *Canaanitish* Woman, to whom he made no answer at first, and then treated her as the Creature he was speaking of [* here *Molinos* is beside his Text.]

39. And although at this time the Lord will not abandon thee, because it would be impossible to live one moment without his help, yet the succour will be so secret that thy Soul will not know it, nor be capable of hope and consolation; nay, it will seem to be without remedy; suffering, like condemned persons, the pains of Hell, *(Circumdederunt me dolores mortis, & pericula inferni invenerunt me,* (Ps. 114) and it would change 'em, as such, with a violent Death, which would be a great comfort; but (like those) the end of those afflictions and bitternesses will seem impossible.

40. But if thou, O blessed Soul, should'st know how much thou art beloved and defended by that Divine Lord, in the midst of thy living torments, thou wouldst find 'em so sweet, that it would be necessary that God should work a Miracle, to let thee live. Be constant, O happy Soul, be constant and of good courage; for however intolerable thou art to thy self, yet thou wilt be protected, inriched, and beloved by that greatest Good, as if he had nothing else to do, than to lead thee to Perfection, by the highest steps of love: and if thou do'st not turn away but preseverest constantly, without leaving off thy undertaking, know, that thou offerest to God the most accepted Sacrifice; so, that if this Lord were capable of pain, he would find no ease till he has completed this loving Union with thy Soul.

41. If from the Chaos of Nothing, his Omnipotence has produced so many wonders, what will he do in thy Soul, created after his own Image and Likeness, if thou keepest constant quiet, and resigned, with a true knowledge of thy Nothing? Happy Soul, which, even when 'tis disturbed, afflicted and disconsolated, keeps steady there within, without going forth

to declare exteriour Comfort.

42. Afflict not thy self too much, and with inquietude, because these sharp Martyrdoms may continue; persevere in Humility, and go not out of thy self to seek aid; for all the good consists in being silent, suffering, and holding patience with rest and resignation: there will thou find the Divine strength to overcome so hard a warfare: he is within thee that fightest for thee: and he is strength it self.

43. When thou shalt come to this painful state of fearful desolation, weeping and lamentation are not forbidden thy Soul, whilest in the upper part of it, it keeps resigned. Who can bear the Lord's heavy hand without tears and Lamentation? That great Champion *Job*, even he lamented; so did Christ our Lord, in his forsakings: but their weepings were accompanied with resignation.

44. Afflict not thy self, though God do crucifie thee and make tryal of thy fidelity; imitate the Woman of Canaan, who being rejected and injured, did importune and persevere, humbling her self and following him, though she were treated as she was. It is necessary to drink the cup and not go back: if the scales were taken from thine eyes, as they were from St. Paul's, thou would'st see the necessity of suffering and glory, as he did; esteeming more the being Crucified, than being an Apostle.

45. Thy good luck consists not in injoying, but in suffering with quiet and resignation. St. Teresa appeared after her death to a certain Soul, and told it, that she had only been rewarded for her pain; but had not received one dram of reward for so many Extasies and Revelations and Comforts that she had here enjoyed in this World.

46. Although this painful martyrdom of horrible desolation and passive purgation be so tremendous, that with reason it hast gotten the name of Hell amongst mystick Divines, (because it seems impossible to be able to live a moment with so grievous a torment; so that with great reason it may be said, that he that suffers it, lives dying, and dying lives a lingring death) yet know, that it is necessary to endure it, to arrive at the sweet, joyous and abundant riches of high contemplation and loving union: and there has been no holy Soul, which has not passed through this spiritual martyrdom and painful torment. St. Gregory the Pope, in the two last Months of his Life; St. Francis of Assize two years and a half; St. Mary Maudlin of Pazzi five years; St. Rose of Peru fifteen years; and after such miracles, as made the world amazed, St. Dominick suffer'd it even till half an hour of his happy *exit*.

SECTION SIX:

47. The other more profitable and meritorious martyrdom in Souls already advanced in perfection and deep contemplation, is, a fire of divine

love, which burns the soul and makes it painful with the same love: sometimes the absence of its beloved afflicts it; sometimes the sweet, ardent and welcome weight of the loving and divine Presence torments it: This sweet martyrdom always makes it sigh sometimes if it enjoys and has its beloved, for the pleasure of having him; so that is cannot contain it self; other times, if he does not manifest himself, through the ardent anxiety of seeking, finding and enjoying him: all this is panting, suffering and dying for love.

48. O that thou could'st but come to conceive the contrariety of accidents that an inamour'd Soul suffers! the combate so terrible and strong on one side; so sweet and melting and amiable on the other! the martyrdom so piercing and sharp with which love torments it; and the cross so painful and sweet withal, without ever being in the mind of getting free from it whil'st thou liv'st!

49. Just so much as light and love increases, just so much increases the grief in seeing that good absent, which it loves so well. To feel it near it self is enjoyment; and never to have done knowing and possessing, it, consumes its life: it has food and drink near its mouth, whil'st it wants either, and cannot be satisfied: it sees it self swallowed up and drown'd in a sea of love, whil'st the powerful hand that is able to save it, is near it; and yet doth not do it; nor doth it know when he will come, who it so much does desire.

50. Sometimes it hears the inward voice of its beloved, which courts and calls it; and a soft and delicate whisper, which goes forth from the secret of the Soul, where it abides, which pierces it strongly, even like to melt and dissolve it, in seeing how near it hath him within it self, and yet how far off from it, whil'st it cannot come to possess him. This intoxicates t, imbases it, scares it, and fills it with unsatisfiableness: and therefore love is said to be as strong as death, whil'st it kills just as that doth.

SECTION SEVEN: *Inward Mortification and Perfect Resignation are necessary for obtaining Internal Peace.*

60. The most subtle Arrow that is shot at us from Nature, is, to induce us to that which is unlawful, with a pretence, that is may be necessary and useful. O how many Souls have suffer'd themselves to be lead away, and have lost the spirit by this guilded Cheat! Thou wilt never tast the delicious Manna [*Quod nemo novit, nisi qui accipit*, (Apoc. ch. 2.) unless thou dost perfectly overcome thy self even to die in thy self; because he who endeavours not to die to his Passions, is not well disposed to receive the Gift of Understanding, without the infusion whereof it is impossible for him to go in into himself and be changed in his Spirit; and therefore those that keep without having nothing of it.

52. Never disquiet thy self for any accident: for inquietude is the door by

which the Enemy gets into the Soul to rob it of its peace.

53. Resign and deny thy self wholly; for though true self-denial is harsh at the beginning, 'tis easie in the middle and becomes most sweet in the end.

54. Thou wilt find thy self far from Perfection, if thou dost not find God in every thing.

55. Know that pure, perfect and essential Love consists in the Cross, in self-denial and resignation, in perfect humility, in poverty of spirit, and in a mean opinion of thy self.

56. In the time of strong temptation, desertion and desolation, 'tis necessary for thee to get close into thy center, that thou may'st only look at and contemplate God, who keeps his throne and his abode in the bottom of thy Soul.

57. Thou wilt find impatience and bitterness of heart to grow from the depth of sensible, empty and mortified love.

58. True love is known, with its effects, when the Soul is profoundly humbled, and desires to be truly mortified and despised.

59. Many there be, who, however they have been dedicated to Prayer, yet have no relish of God; because in the end of their Prayers, they are neither mortified nor attend upon God any longer: for obtaining that peaceable and continual attending, 'tis necessary to get a great purity of mind and heart, great peace of soul, and an universal resignation.

60. To the simple and the mortified, the recreation of the senses is a sort of death: they never go to it, unless compelled by necessity and edification of their neighbours.

61. The bottom of our soul, you will know, is the place of our happiness. There the Lord shews us wonders: there we ingulf and lose our selves in the immense ocean of his infinite goodness, in which we keep fixt and unmoveable. There, there resides the incomparable fruition of our Soul and that eminent and sweet rest of it. An humble and resign'd Soul, which is come to this bottom, seeks no more than meerly to please God, and the holy and loving spirit teaches it every thing with his sweet and enlivening unction.

62. Amongst the Saints there are some gigantick ones, who continually suffer with patience indispositions of body, of which God takes great care. But high and sovereign is their gift, who by the strength of the Holy Ghost, suffer both internal and external crosses with content and resignation. This is that sort of holiness so much the more rare, as it is more precious in the sight of God. The spiritual ones, which walk this way, are rare: because there are few in the world, who do totally deny themselves, to follow Christ crucified, with simpleness and bareness of spirit, through the loansom and thorny ways of the Cross, without making reflexions upon themselves.

63. A Life of Self denial is above all the Miracles of the Saints; and it

doth not know whether it be alive or dead; lost or gained; whether it agrees or resists: this is the trne resigned Life. But although it should be a long time before thou comest to this state, and thou should'st think not to have made one step towards it, yet affright not thy self at this, for God uses to bestow upon a Soul that Blessing in one moment, which was denied it for many years before.

64. He that desires to suffer blindfold, without the comfort of God or the creatures, is gotten too far onwards to be able to resist unjust accusations which his enemies make against him, even in the most dreadful and interior desolation.

65. The spiritual man that lives by God, and in him, is inwardly contented in the midst of his adversities; because the Cross and Affliction are his Life and Delight.

66. Tribulation is a great treasure, wherewith God honours those that be his, in this life: therefore evil men are necessary for those that are good; and so are the Devils themselves, which by afflicting us do try to ruine us: but instead of doing us harm, they do us the greatest good imaginable.

67. There must be tribulation to make a man's life acceptable to God; without it, 'tis like the Body without the Soul, the Soul without Grace, the Earth without the Sun.

68. With the wind of tribulation God separates, in the floor of the Soul, the Chaff from the Corn.

69. When God crucifies in the inmost part of the Soul, no creature is able to comfort it; nay, comforts are but grievous and bitter crosses to it. And if it be well-instructed in the laws and discipline of the ways of pure love, in the time of great desolation and inward troubles, it ought not to seek abroad among the creatures for comfort, nor lament it self with them, nor will it be able to read Spiritual Books: because this is a secret way of getting at a distance from suffering.

70. Those Souls are to be pitied, who cannot find in their hearts to believe, that Tribulation and Suffering is their greatest Blessing. They who are perfect ought always to be desirous of dying and suffering, being always in a state of death and suffering: vain is the man who doth not suffer: because he is born to toyl and suffering; but much more the Friends and Elect of God.

71. Undeceive thy self, and believe, that in order to thy Soul's being totally transformed with God, it is necessary for it to be lost and be denied in its life, sense, knowledge, and power; and to die living, and not living; dying, and not dying; suffering, and not suffering; resigning up, and not resigning up it self, without reflecting upon any thing.

72. Perfection, in its followers, receives not its glories but by Fire and Martyrdom, Griefs, Torments, Punishments and Contempt, suffered and endured with gallantry and courage; and he that would have some place to

set his feet on and rest himself, and does not go beyond the reason of reason and of sense, will never get into the secret cabinet of knowledge, though by reading he may chance to get a taste and relish the understanding of it.

SECTION EIGHT: *Pursues the Same Matter*

73. You must know, that the Lord will not manifest himself in thy Soul, till it be denied in it self, and dead in its senses and powers: nor will it ever come to this state, till being perfectly resigned, it resolves to be with God all alone; making an equal account of Gifts and Contempts, Light and Darkness, Peace and War. In summ, that the Soul may arrive at perfect quietness and supreme internal peace, it ought first to die in it self, and live only in God and for him: and the more dead it shall be in it self, the more shall it know God: but if it doth not mind this continual denying of it self and internal mortification, it will never arrive at this state, nor preserve God within it; and then it will be continually subject to accidents and passions of the mind, such as are judging, murmuring, resenting, excusing, defending, to keep its honour and reputation, which are enemies to Perfection, Peace, and the Spirit.

74. Know that the diversity of states amongst those that be spiritual, consists only in dying all alike; but in the happy, which die continually, God hath his honour, his blessing and delights here below.

75. Great is the difference which is between doing, suffering, and dying; doing is delightful and belongs to beginners; suffering, with desire, belongs to those who are proficients; dying always in themselves, belongs to those who are accomplished and perfect; of which number there are very few in the world.

76. How happy wilt thou be, if thou hast no other thought, but to die in thy self! thou wilt then become not only victorious over thine enemies, but also over thy self: in which victory thou wilt certainly find pure love, perfect peace, and divine wisdom.

77. It is impossible for a man to be able to think and live mystically in a simple understanding of the divine and infused wisdom, if he does not first die in himself by the total denying of sense, and the reasonable appetite.

78. The true lesson of the spiritual man, and that which thou oughtest to learn, is, to leave all things in their place, and not meddle with any, but what thy office may bind thee to: because the Soul which leaves every thing to find God, doth then begin to have all in the eternity it seeks.

79. Some Souls there are, who seek repose: others without seeking have the pleasure of it; others have a pleasure in pain; and others seek it. The first do as good as nothing; the second are in the way towards it; the third run, and the last fly.

80. The disesteem of delights, and the counting of 'em torment, is the

property of a truly mortified man.

81. Enjoyment and Internal Peace are the Fruits of the Spirit Divine; and no man gets 'em into his possession, if in the closet of his soul he is not a resigned man.

82. Thou seest that the displeasures of the good pass presently away; but for all that endeavour never to have 'em, nor to stop in 'em: for they damnifie thy health, disturb thy reason, and disquiet thy spirit.

83. Amongst other holy Counsels which thou must observe, remember well this that follows: Look not upon other mens faults, but thine own: keep silence with a continued internal conversation: mortifie thy self in all things and at all hours, and by this means thou wilt get free from many imperfections, and make thy self Commander of great Vertues.

84. Mortifie thy self in not judging ill of any body at any time; because the suspicion of thy neighbour disturbs the purity of heart, discomposes it, brings the Soul out and takes away its repose.

85. Never wilt thou have perfect resignation, if thou mind'st humane respects, and reflectest upon the little idol of what people say. The Soul that goes by the inward way, will soon lose it self, if once it come to look at reason amongst the creatures, and in commerce and conversation with 'em. There is no other reason, than not to look at reason; but to imagine that God permits grievances to fall on us, to humble and annihilate us and make us live wholly resigned.

86. Behold how God makes greater account of a Soul that lives internally resigned, than of another that doth miracles, even to the raising of the dead.

87. Many Souls there are, which, though they exercise Prayer, yet because they are not mortified, are always imperfect and full of self-love.

88. Hold it for a true maxim, that no body can do a grievance or injury to a Soul despised by it self, and one that is nothing in its own account.

89. Finally, be of hope, suffer, be silent, and patient: let nothing affright thee: all of it will have an time to end: God only is he that is unchangeable: patience brings a man in every thing. He that hath God, hath all things; and he that hath him not, hath nothing.

SECTION NINE: *For the obtaining of Internal Peace, 'tis necessary for the Soul to know its misery.*

90. If the Soul should not fall into some faults, it would never come to understand its own misery, though it hears men speak and reads spiritual Books; nor can it ever obtain precious peace, if it do not first know its own miserable weakness: because there the remedy is difficult, where there is no clear knowledge of the defect. God will suffer in thee sometimes one fault, sometimes another, that by this knowledge of thy self, seeing thee so often

fallen, thou may'st believe that thou art a meer nothing; in which knowledge and belief true peace and perfect humility is founded: and that thou may'st the better search into thy mystery and see what thou art, I will try to undeceive thee in some of thy manifold imperfections.

91. Thou art so quick and nice, that it may be if thou dost but trip as thou walkest or findest thy way molested, thou feelest even Hell it self: if thou are denied thy due or thy pleasure opposed, thou presently briskest up with a warm resentment of it. If though spiest a fault in thy neighbour, instead of pitying him, and thinking that thou they self art liable to the same failing, thou indiscreetly reprovest him; if thou seest a thing convenient for thee and canst not compass it, thou growest sad and full of sorrow; if thou receivest a slight injury from thy neighbour, thou chidest at him and complainest for it: insomuch that for any trifle thou art inwardly and outwardly discomposed and losest thy self.

92. Thou would'st be penitent, but with another's patience; and if the impatience still continues, thou layest the fault with much pains upon thy companion, without considering, that thou art intolerable to thy self: and when the rancour is over, thou cunningly dost return to make thy self vertuous, giving documents and relating spiritual sayings with artifice of wit, without mending thy past faults. Although thou willingly dost condemn thy self, reproving thy faults before others, yet this thou dost more to justifie thy self with him that sees thy faults, that thou may'st return again afresh to the former esteem of thy self, than through any effect of perfect humility.

93. Other times thou dost subtilly alledge, that is it not through fault but zeal of justice, that thou complainest of thy neighbour. Thou believest for the most part that thou art vertuous, constant and couragious, even to the giving up thy life into the tyrant's hand, solely for the sake of divine love; yet thou canst scarce hear the least word of anger but presently thou dost afflict and trouble and disquiet thy self. These are all industrious engines of self-love and the secret pride of thy soul. Know therefore that self-love reigns in thee, and that from purchasing this precious peace, that is thy greatest hindrance.

SECTION TEN: *In which is shewed and discovered what is the false humility, and what the true; with the effects of 'em.*

94. Thou must know that there are two sorts of humility; one false and counterfeit, the other true. The false one is theirs, who, like water which must mount upward, receive an external fall and artificial submission, to rise up again immediately. These avoid esteem and honour, that so they may be took to be humble; they say of themselves, that they are very evil, that they many be thought good; and though they know their own misery, yet they are loth that other folks should know it. This is dissembled humility, and

feigned, and nothing but secret pride.

95. Theirs is the true humility, which have gotten a perfect habit of it; these never think of it, but judge humbly of themselves; they do things with courage and patience; they live and dye in God; they mind not themselves nor the Creatures; they are constant and quiet in all things; they suffer molestation with joy, desiring more of it, that they may imitate their dear and despised Jesus; they covet to be reputed trifles and sport by the World; they are contented with what God alots 'em, and are convinced of their faults with a pleasing shame; they are not humbled by the counsel of Reason, but by the affection of the Will; there is no honour that they look after, nor injury to disturb 'em.; no trouble to vex 'em; no prosperity to make 'em proud; because they are always immovable in their Nothing, and in themselves with absolute peace.

96. And that thou mayst be acquainted with interiour and true Humility, know, that it doth not consist in external Acts, in taking the lowest place, in going poor in cloaths, in speaking submissively, in shutting the eyes, in affectionate sighing, nor in condemning thy ways, calling thy self miserable, to give others to understand that thou art humble: It consists only in the contempt of thy self, and the desire to be despised, with a low and profound knowledge, without concerning thy self, whether thou art esteemed humble or no, though an Angel should reveal such a thing to thee.

97. The torrent of Light wherewith the Lord with his Graces inlightens the soul, doth two things: It discovers the Greatness of God, and at the same time the Soul knows its own stench and misery, insomuch, that no Tongue is able to express the depth in which it is overwhelmed, being desirous that every one should know its Humility, and 'tis so far from vain-glory and Complacency, as it sees that Grace of God to be the meer Goodness of him, and nothing but his Mercy, which is pleased to take pity on it.

98. Thou shalt never be hurt by Men or Devils, but by thy self, thy own proper Pride, and the violence of thy Passions; take heed of thy self, for thou of thy self, art the greatest Devil of all to thy self.

99. Have no Mind to be esteemed, when God incarnate was called Fool, Drunkard, and said to have a Devil. O the Folly of Christians! that we should be willing to enjoy Happiness, without being willing to imitate him on the Cross, in Reproaches, Humility, Poverty, and in other Vertues!

100. The truly humble Man is at rest and ease in his Heart; there he stands the Tryal of God, and Men, and the Devil himself, above all reason and discretion possessing himself in Peace and Quietness, looking for, with all Humility, the pure pleasure of God, as well in Life as Death: Things without do no more disquiet him, than if they never were. The Cross to him, and even Death it self, are Delights, though he make no such shew

outwardly: But oh! who do we speak of? for few there are of these sort of humble Men in the whole World!

101. Hope thou, and desire, and suffer, and dye without any Bodies knowing it; for herein consists the humber and perfect Love. O how much Peace wilt thou find in thy Soul, if thou dost profoundly humble thy self, and even hugg Contempt!

102. Thou wilt never be perfectly hnmble, though thou knowest thy own Misery, unless thou desirest that all Men should know it: then thou wilt avoid Praises, embrace Injuries, despise every thing, that makes a fair shew, even to thine own self: and if any Tribulation come upon thee, blame none for it; but Judge that it comes from God's Hand, as the Giver of every Good.

103. If thou would'st bear thy Neighbours faults, cast thine Eyes upon thine own: and if thou thinkest to thy self, that thou hast made any Progress in Perfection by thy self, know that thou art not humble at all, nor hast yet made one step in the way of the Spirit.

104. The degrees of Humility, are the qualities of a Body in the Grave; that is, to be in the lowest place, buried like one that's dead, to stink, and be corrupted to it self, to be dust, and nothing in ones own account; finally, if thou would'st be Blessed, learn to despise thy self, and to be despised by others.

SECTION ELEVEN: *Maxims to know a simple, humble, and true Heart.*

105. Encourage thy self to be Humble, embracing Tribulations as Instruments of thy Good; rejoyce in Contempt, and desire that God may be thy only Refuge, Comfort and Protector.

106. None, let him be never so great in this World, can be greater than he that is in the eye and favour of God: and therefore the truly humble Man despises whatever there is in the World, even to himself, and puts his only trust and repose in God.

107. The truly humble Man suffers quietly and patiently internal troubles, and he is the Man that makes great way in a little time, like one that sails before the Wind.

108. The truly humble Man finds God inall things; so that whatever contempt, injury or affront comes to him by means of the Creatures, he receives it with great peace and quiet Internal, as sent from the Divine Hand, and loves greatly the instrument with which the Lord tryes him.

109. He is not yet arrived at profound Humility that is taken with Praise, though he does not desire it, nor seek it, but rather avoids it: because to an humble Heart praises are bitter crosses although it be wholly quiet and immovable.

110. He has no internal Humility who doth not abhor himself, with a

mortal, but withal a peaceable and quiet hatred: But he will never come to possess this treasure, that has not a low and profound knowledge of his own vileness, rottenness and misery.

111. He that is upon excuses and replies, has not a simple and humble heart, especially if he dost this with his Superiours: because replies grow from a secret pride that reigns in the Soul; and from thence the total ruine of it.

112. Perfidiousness supposes little submission, and this less humility; and both together they are the fewel of inquietude, discord and disturbance.

113. The humble heart is not disquieted by imperfections, though these do grieve it to the Soul; because they are against its loving Lord: nor is he concerned that he cannot do great things; for he always stands in his own Nothing and Misery; nay, he wonders at himself, that he can do any thing of Vertue, and presently thanks the Lord for it, with a true knowledge that it is God that doth all, and remains dissatisfied with what he does himself.

114. The truly humble man, though he see all, yet he looks upon nothing to judge it, because he judge ill only of himself.

115. The truly humble man doth always find an excuse to defend him that mortifies him, and least in a sound intention: Who therefore would be angry with a Man of good intention?

116. So much (nay more) doth false humility displease God, as true Pride does; because that is Hypocrisy besides.

117. The truly humble Man, though every thing falls out contrary to him, is neither disquieted nor afflicted at it; because he is prepared, and thinks he deserves no less; he is not disquieted under troublesome Thoughts, wherewith the Devil seeks to torment him, nor under temptations, tribulations and desertions, but rather acknowledges his unworthiness, and is affected that the Lord chastises him by the Devil's means, though he be a vile instrument; all he suffers seems nothing to him, and he never doth a thing that he thinks worth any great matter.

118. He that is arrived at perfect and inward Humility, although he be disturbed at nothing, as one that abhors himself, because he knows his imperfection in every thing, his ingratitude and his misery, yet he suffers a great Cross in induring himself. This is the sign to know true humility of Heart by. But the happy Soul which is gotten to this holy hatred of it self, lives overwhelmed, drowned and swallowed up in the depth of its own Nothing; out of which the Lord raises him by communicating Divine Wisdom to him, and filling him with Light, Peace, Tranquility and Love.

SECTION TWELVE: *Inward solitude is that which chiefly brings a Man to the purchase of Internal Peace.*

119. Know that although exteriour Solitude doth much assist for the obtaining internal Peace, yet the Lord did not mean this, when he spake by

his Prophet, (Hos. 2. 14.) *I will bring her into solitude, and speak privately to her.*
But he meant the interiour Solitude, which joyntly conduces to the
obtaining the precious Jewel of Peace Internal. Internal Solitude consists in
the foregetting all the Creatures, in disengaging ones self from 'em, in a
perfect nakedness of all the affections, desires, thoughts, and ones own will.
This is the true Solitude where the Soul reposes with a sweet and inward
serenity in the arms of its cheifest good.

120. O what infinite room is there in a Soul that is arrived at this divine
Solitude! O what inward, what retired, what secret, what spacious, what vast
distances are there within a happy Soul that is once come to be truly
Solitary! There the Lord converses and communicates himself, inwardly
with the Soul: there he fills it with himself, because it is empty; cloaths it
with Light, and with his Love, because it is naked; lifts it up, because 'tis
low; and unites it with himself, and transforms it, because it is alone.

121. O delightful Solitude, and Gifer of eternal Blessings! O Mirrour, in
which the eternal Father is always beheld! There is great reason to call thee
Solitude; for thou art so much alone, that there is scarce a Soul that looks
after thee, that loves and knows thee. O Divine Lord! How is it that Souls
do not go from Earth to this Glory! How come they to lose so great a
good, through the only love and desire of created things! Blessed Soul, how
happy wilt thou be, if thou do'st but leave all for God! seek him only,
breathe after none but him, let him only have thy sighs. Desire nothing, and
then nothing can trouble thee; and if thou do'st desire any good, how
spiritual soever it be, let it be in such a manner, that thou mayest not be
disquieted, if thou missest it.

122. If, with this liberty, thou wilt give thy Soul to God, taken off from
the World, free and alone, thou wilt be the happiest creature upon Earth;
because the most High has his secret habitation in this holy Solitude; in this
Desart and Paradise, is enjoyed the conversation of God, and it is only in
this internal Retirement that that marvellous, powerful and divine Voice is
heard.

123. If thou would'st enter into this Heaven of Earth, forget every care
and every thought; get out of thy self, that the love of God may live in thy
Soul.

124. Live as much as ever thou canst, abstracted from the Creatures;
dedicate thy self wholly to thy Creator, and offer thy self in Sacrifice with
Peace and quietness of Spirit: Know, that the more the Soul disrobes it self,
the more way it makes into this interiour Solitude, and becomes cloathed
with God, and the more lonesome and empty of it self the Soul gets to be,
the more the divine Spirit fills it.

125. There is not a more blessed Life than a solitary one; because in this
happy Life, God gives himself all to the Creature, and the Creature all to
God by an intimate and sweet union of Love. O how few are there that

come to relish this true Solitude!

126. To make the Soul truly Solitary, it ought to forget all the Creatures, and even it self; otherwise it will never be able to make any near approach to God. Many men leave and forsake all things, but they do not leave their own liking, their own will, and themselves; and therefore these truly solitary ones are so few; wherefore if the Soul does not get off from its own Appetite and Desire, from its own will, from spiritual Gifts, and from repose even in the Spirit it self, it never can arrive at this high felicity of internal Solitude.

127. Go on, blessed Soul! go on, without stop, towards this blessedness of internal Solitude: See how God calls thee to enter into thy inward Center, where he will renew thee, change thee, fill thee, cloath thee, and shew thee a new and Heavenly Kingdom, full of joy, peace, content and serenity.

SECTION THIRTEEN: *In which is shewed what infused and passive Contemplation, is, and its wonderful Effects.*

128. You must know, that when once the Soul is habituated to internal Recollection, and acquired Contemplation, that we have spoken of; when once 'tis mortified, and desires wholly to be denied its Appetites; when once it efficaciously embraces internal and external Mortification, and is willing to dye heartily to its passions and its own ways, then God uses to take it alone by it self, and raise it more then it knows, to a compleat repose, where he sweetly and inwardly infuses in it his Light, his Love and his Strength, inkindling and inflaming it with a true disposition to all manner of Vertue.

129. There the Divine Spouse, suspending its Powers, puts it to sleep in a most sweet and pleasant rest: There it sleeps, and quietly receives and enjoys (without knowing it) what it enjoys, with a most lovely and charming Calm: There the Soul raised and lifted up to this passive State, becomes united to its greatest Good, without costing it any trouble or pains for this Union: There in that supream Region, and sacred Temple of the Soul, that greatest Good takes its Complacency, manifests it self, and creates a relish from the Creature, in a way above Sense and all humane understanding: There also only the pure Spirit, who is God, (the purity of the Soul being uncapable of sensible things) rules it, and gets the mastership of it, communicating to it its illustrations, and those Sentiments which are necessary for the most pure and perfect Union.

130. The Soul coming to it self again from these sweet and divine Embracings, becomes rich in light and love, and a mighty esteem of the divine Greatness, and the knowledge of its own Misery, finding it self all changed divinely, and disposed to embrace, to suffer, and to practice perfect Vertue.

131. A simple, pure, infused, and perfect Contemplation, therefore is a

known and inward manifestation which God gives of himself, of his goodness, of his Peace, of his sweetness, whose object is God, pure, unspeakable, abstracted from all particular thoughts, within an inward silence: but it is God delights us, God that draws us, God that sweetly raises us in a spiritual and pure manner, an admirable gift, which the divine Majesty bestows to whom he will, as he will, and when he will, and for what time he will, though the state of this Life be rather a state of the cross of Patience, of humility, and of suffering, than of enjoying.

132. Never wilt thou enjoy this divine Nectar, till thou art advanced in Vertue and inward Mortification; till thou doest heartily endeavour to fix in thy Soul a great Peace, silence, forgetfulness and internal solitude: How is it possible to hear the sweet, inward and powerful Voice of God in the midst of the noise and tumults of the Creatures? And how can the pure spirit be heard in the midst of Considerations and discourses of Artifice? If the Soul will not continually dye in it self, denying it self to all these Materiallities and satisfactions, the Contemplation can be no more but a meer vanity, a vain complacency and Presumption.

SECTION FOURTEEN: *Pursues the Same Matter*

133. God doth not always communicate himself with equal abundance in this sweetest and infused Contemplation: sometimes he grants this Grace more than he doth at other times; and sometimes he expects not that the Soul should be so dead and denied, because this Gift being his meer Grace, he gives it when he pleases, and as he pleases; so that no general rule can be made of it, nor any rate set to his Divine greatness: nay, by means of this very Contemplation be comes to deny it to annihilate and dye.

134. Sometimes the Lord gives greater light to the understanding; sometimes greater love to the will. There is no need here for the Soul to take any pains or trouble; it must receive what God gives it, and rest united, as he will have it; because His Majesty is Lord, and in the very time that he lays it asleep, he possesses and fills it, and works in it powerfully and sweetly, without any industry or knowledge of its own: insomuch, that before ever it is aware of this so great Mercy, it is gained, convinced, and changed already.

135. The Soul which is in this happy state, hath two things to avoid, the activity of human Spirit, and interestedness: Our humane Spirit is unwilling to dye in it self, but loveth to be doing and discoursing after its way, being in Love with its own Actions. A Man had need to have a great fidelity, and devesting himself of selfishness, to get a perfect and passive Capacity of the Divine Influences; the continual habits of operating freely, which it has, are a hindrance to its annihilation.

136. The second is interestedness in contemplation it self: Thou must

therefore procure in thy Soul a perfect devesting of all which is not God, without seeking any other end or interest, within or without, but the Divine Will.

137. In a word, the manner that thou must use, on thy part, to fit thy self for this pure, passive, and perfect Prayer, is, a total and absolute consignment of thy self into the hands of God, with a perfect submission to his most holy Will, to be busied according to his Pleasure and Disposition, with a perfect resignation.

138. Thou must know, that few be the Souls which arrive at this infused and passive Prayer; because few of 'em are capable of these divine influences with a total nakedness and death of their own activity and Powers, those only which feel it, know it so, that this perfect nakedness is acquired (by the help of God's Grace) by a continual and inward mortification, dying to all its own inclinations and desires.

139. At no time must thou look at the effects which are wrought in thy Soul, but especially herein; because it would be a hindrance to the divine operations, which enrich it, so to do: all that thou hast to do is to pant after indifference, resignation, forgetfulness, and, without thy being sensible of it; the greatest good will leave in thy Soul a fit disposition for the practice of vertue, an true love of the Cross of thy own contempt, of thy Annihilation, and greater and stronger desires still of thy greater Perfection, and the most pure and affective Union.

SECTION FIFTEEN: *Of the two means, whereby the Soul ascends up to infused Contemplation, with the Explication of what and how many the steps of it are.*

140. The means whereby the Soul ascends to the felicity of Contemplation and Affective Love, are two; the Pleasure, and the Desires of it. God uses at first to fill the Soul with sensible Pleasures; because 'tis so frail and miserable, that, without this preventive Consolation, it cannot take wing towards the fruition of Heavenly things. In this first step it is disposed by Contrition, and is exercised in Repentance, meditating upon the Redeemer's Passion, rooting out diligently all worldly desires and vicious Courses of Life: because the Kingdom of Heaven suffers violence, and the faint-heart, the delicate never conquer it, but those that use violence and force with themselves.

141. The second is the Desires. The more the things of Heaven are delighted in, the more they are desired; and from thence there do ensue upon spiritual Pleasures, desires of enjoying heavenly and divine Blessings, and contempt of worldly ones. From these desires arises the inclination of following Christ our Lord, who said, *I am the way,* (St. John 14. 6) the steps of his imitation, by which a Man must go up, are Charity, Humility, Meekness, Patience, Poverty, Self-contempt, the Cross, Prayer, and

Mortification.

142. The steps of infused Contemplation are three. The first is Satiety. When the soul is fill'ed with God, it conceives a Hatred to all worldly things; then 'tis quiet and satisfied only with Divine Love.

143. The second is intoxication. And this step is an excess of Mind, and an Elevation of Soul, arising from Divine Love and satiety of it.

144. The third is Security. This step turns out all fear: the soul is so drencht with love divine, and resigned up in such a manner to the divine good pleasure, that it would go willingly to Hell, if it did but know it so to be the will of the most high. In this step it feels such a certain Bond of the divine Union, that it seems to it an impossible thing, to be separated from its beloved, and his infinite Treasure.

145. There are six other steps of Contemplation, which are these, Fire, Union, Elevation, Illumination, Pleasure, and Repose. With the first the Soul is inkindled, and being inkindled, is anointed; being anointed, is raised; being raised, Contemplates; Contemplating, it receives Pleasure; and receiving Pleasure, it finds repose. By these steps the soul rises higher, being abstracted and experienced in the Spiritual and Internal way.

146. In the first step, which is Fire, the Soul is illustrated, by the means of a divine and ardent ray, in kindling the affections divine, and drying up those which are but humane. The second is the Unction, which is a sweet and spiritual Liquor, which diffusing it self all the Soul over, teaches it, strengthens it, and disposes it to receive and contemplate the divine truth: and sometimes it extends even to nature it self, corroborating it by patience, with a sensible pleasure that seems celestial.

147. The third is the Elevation of the Inner Man over it self, that it may get fittest to the clear fountain of pure love.

148. The fourth step, which is Illumination, is an infused knowledge, whereby the Soul contemplates sweetly the divine truth, rising still from one clearness to another, from one light to another, from knowledge to knowledge, begin guided by the Spirit Divine.

149. The fifth is a Savoury Pleasure of the divine sweetness, issuing forth from the plentiful and precious fountain of the Holy Ghost.

150. The sixth is a sweet and Admirable tranquility, arising from the conquest of Fightings within, and frequent Prayer; and this, *very, very* few have Experience of. Here the abundance of Joy, and Peace is so great, that the soul seems to be in a sweet sleep, solacing and reposing it self in the Divine breast of Love.

151. Many other steps of Contemplation there are, as Extasies, Raptures, Melting, *Delinquium's*, Glee, Kisses, Embraces, Exultation, Union, Transformation, Expousing, and Matrimony, which I omit to explain, to give no occasion to Speculation: And because there are whole Books which treat of these Points; though they are all for him who finds nothing of 'em,

any more than a blind Man doth of Colour, or a deaf Man of Musick. In a word, by these steps we get up to the Chamber and repose of the pacifick King and the true *Solomon.*

SECTION SIXTEEN: *Signs to know the Inner Man, and the Mind that's purged*

152. The Signs to know the Inner Man by, are four. The first, If the understanding produce not other Thoughts than those which stir up to the light of Faith; and the Will is so habituated, that it begets no other Acts of Love than of God, and in order to him. The second, If, when he ceases from an External Work, in which he was employed, the Understanding and the Will are presently and easily turned to God. The third, if in entring, upon Prayer, he forgets all outward things, as if he had not seen nor used 'em. The fourth, If he carries himself orderly towards outward things, as if he were entring into the World again, fearing to embroil himself in Business, and naturally abhorring it, unless when Charity requires it of him.

153. Such a Soul as this is free from the outward Man, and easily enters into the interiour solitude, where it sees none but God and it self in him: loving him with quiet and peace and true Love. There in that secret Center God is kindly speaking to it, teaching it a new Kingdom, and true Peace and Joy.

154. This Spiritual, abstracted and retired Soul hath its Peace no more broken, though outwardly it may meet with Combats; because through the infinite distance, tempests do never reach to that serenest Heaven within, where pure and perfect Love resides; and though sometimes it may be naked, forsaken, fought against and desolate, this is only the fury of the storm, which threatens and rages no where but without.

155. This secret Love within, hath four effects: The first is called Illumination, which is a savoury and experimental Knowledge of the greatness of God, and of its own nothing. The second is Inflammation, which is an ardent desire of being burnt, like the *Salamander*, in this kind and divine fire. The third is Sweetness, which is a peaceable, joyful, sweet and intimate fruition. The fourth, is a swallowing up of the Powers in God; by which immersion the Soul is so much drencht and filled with God, that it can't any longer seek, or will any thing, but its greatest and infinite good.

156. From this fullest satiety, two effects arise. The first is, a great Courage to suffer for God. The second is, a certain hope or assurance that it can never lose him, nor be separated from him.

157. Here in this internal retirement, the beloved Jesus hath his Paradise, to whom we may go up, standing and conversing on the Earth. And if thou desirest to know who he is, who is altogether drawn to this inward retirement, with enlightened Exemplification in God, I tell thee, it is he that in adversity, in discomfort of Spirit, and in the want of necessities stands

firm and unshaken. These constant and inward Souls are outwardly naked and wholly diffused in God, whom they continually do Contemplate: they have no spot; they live in God and of himself; they shine brighter than a thousand Suns; they are beloved by the Son of God; they are the darlings of God the Father, and elect Spouses of the Holy Ghost.

158. By three signs is a mind that is purged, to be known, as St. Thomas says in a Treatise of his. The first sign is diligence, which is a strength of Mind, which banishes all neglect and sloth, that it may be disposed with earnestness and confidence to the pursuit of vertue. The second is severity; which likewise is a strength of Mind against Concupiscence, accompanied with an ardent love of roughness, vileness and holy Poverty. The third is benignity and sweetness of Mind, which drives away all rancour, envy, aversion and hatred against ones neighbour.

159. Till the mind be purged, the affection purified, the memory naked, the understanding brightened, the will denied and set a fire, the Soul can never arrive at the intimate and affective union with God, and therefore because the Spirit of God is purity it self, and light and rest, the Soul, where he intends to make his abode, must have great Purity, Peace, attention and quiet. Finally the precious Gift of a purged Mind, those only have, who with continual diligence do seek Love and retain it, and desire to be reputed the most vile in the World.

SECTION SEVENTEEN: *Of Divine Wisdom*

160. Divine Wisdom is an intellectual and infused knowledge of the divine perfections and things Eternal; which ought rather to be called Contemplation than Speculation. Science is acquired and begets the knowledge of Nature. Wisdom is infused and begets the Knowledge of the Divine Goodness. That desires to know what is not to be attained unto without pains and sweat: This desires not to know what it doth know, although it understands it all. In a word, the Men who are scientifical entertain themselves in the knowledge of the things of the World; and the wise live swallowed up in God himself.

161. Reason enlightened in the Wise is a high and simple elevation of Spirit, whereby he sees, with a clear and sharp sight all that is inferiour to him, and what concerns his Life and Estate. This is that which renders the Soul simple, illustrated, uniform, spiritual, and altogether introverted, and abstracted from every created thing. This moves and draws away with a sweet Violence, the hearts of the humble and teachable, filling them with abundance of sweetness, peace, and pleasantness. Finally, the wise Man says of it, that it brought him all good things at once. *Venerunt mihi omnia bona pariter cum illa*, Wisd. 7. 11.

162. You must know, that the greatest part of Men lives by Opinion,

92

and judges according to the deceivableness of imagination and Sence: but the Man that's wise judges of every thing according to the real verity, which is in it; whose business is to understand, conceive, penetrate into, and transcend every created being, even to himself.

163. 'Tis a great property of a wise Man to do much and say little.

164. Wisdom is discovered in the works and words of the wise; because he being absolute master of all his passions, motions, and affections is know in all his doings, like a quiet and still water, in which wisdom shines with clearness.

165. The understanding of mystical truths is secret and shut up from Men who are purely Scholastical, unless they be humble; because it is the Science of Saints, and none know it but those which heartily love and seek their own Contempt: Therefore the Souls, who by imbracing this means, get to be purely mystical and truly humble, dive even to the profoundest apprehensions of the Divinity: and the more sensually men do live according to flesh and blood, the greater distance are they at from this mystical Science.

166. Ordinarily it is seen that in the man which hath much scholastical and speculative Knowledge, divine Wisdom doth not predominate; yet they make an admirable composition, when they both meet together. The men of Learning, who by God's Mercy have attained to this mystick Science, are worthy of Veneration and Praise in Religion.

167. The external actions of the mystical and wise, which they do rather passively than actively, though, they are a great torment to 'em, yet are ordered prudently by 'em, by number, weight, and measure,

168. The Sermons of Men of Learning, who want the Spirit, though they are made up of divers stories, elegant descriptions, acute discourses, and exquisite Proofs, yet are by no means the word of God; but the word of Men, plated over with false Gold: These Preachers spoil Christians, feeding 'em with wind and vanity, and so they are, both of 'em, void of God.

169. These Teachers feed their Hearers with the wind of hurtful subtilties, giving 'em stones instead of Bread, leaves instead of Fruit, and unsavoury Earth mixt with poisoned Honey instead of true Food. These are they that hunt after honour, raising up an idol of reputation and applause, instead of seeking God's Glory, and the spiritual Edification of Men.

170. Those that preach with Zeal and sincerity, preach for God. Those that preach without 'em, preach for themselves. Those that preach the word of God with spirit, makes it take impression in the Heart; but those that Preach it without spirit, carry it no farther than to the ear.

171. Perfection doth not consist in teaching it, but in doing it; because he is neither the greatest Saint, nor the wisest Man, that knows the Truth most, but he that practices it.

172. 'Tis a constant Maxim, That Divine Wisdom begets Humility; and

that which is acquired by the Learned, begets Pride.

173. Holiness does not consist in forming deep and subtle conceits of the Knowledge and attributes of God, but in the Love of God, and in self-denial. Therefore 'tis frequentlier observed, that Holiness is more amongst the simple, and humble, than among the learned. How many poor old Women are there in the World, which have little or nothing of humane science, but are rich in the love of God! How many Divines do we see that are over head and ears in their vain Wisdom, and yet very bare in things of true light and Charity!

174. Remember that 'tis always good to speak like one that learns, and not like one that knows: Count it a greater Honour to be reputed a meer Ignoramus, than a man of Wisdom and Prudence.

175. However, the Learned, who are purely speculative, have some little Sparks of Spirit, yet these do not fly out from the simple bottom of eminent and divine Wisdom, which hath a mortal hatred to Forms and Species's: the mixing of a little Science is always a hindrance to the eternal, profound, pure, simple, and true Wisdom.

SECTION EIGHTEEN: *Treating of the Same*

176. There are two ways which lead to the knowledg of God. The one remote, the other near: The first is called Speculation; the second, Contemplation. The Learned, who follow Scientifical Speculation by the Sweetness of sensible Discourses, get up to God by this means, as well as they can, that by this help they may be able to love him: But none of those who follow that way which they call Scholastical, ever arrives by that only, to the Mystical Way, or to the Excellence of Union, Transformation, Simplicity, Light, Peace, Tranquility and Love, as he doth, who is brought by the Divine Grace by the mystical way of Contemplation.

177. These men of Learning, who are meerly scholastical, don't know what the Spirit is, nor what it is to be lost in God: nor are they come yet to the taste of the sweet Ambrosia which is in the inmost depth and bottom of the Soul, where it keeps its Throne, and communicates it self with incredible, intimate and delicious affluence: Nay, some there are which do e'en condemn this mystical Science, because they neither do understand nor relish it.

178. The Divine who doth not taste the sweetness of Contemplation, has not other reason to give for it, but because he enters not by the Gate which St. *Paul* points to, when he says, *Si quis inter vos videtur sapiens esse, stultus fiat ut sit sapiens,* I Cor. 3.18. If any one among ye seem to himself to be wise, let him become a fool that he may be wise; let him shew his humility by reputing himself ignorant.

179. 'Tis a general Rule; and also a Maxim in Mystick Theology, That

the Practic ought to be gotten before the Theory. That there ought to be some experimental Exercise of supernatural Contemplation, before the search of the knowledge, and an enquiry after the full apprehension of it.

180. Although the mystical Science does commonly belong to the humble and simple, yet notwithstanding that, men of Learning are not uncapable of it, if they do not seek themselves nor set any great value upon their own artificial knowledge; but more, if they can forget it, as if they never had it, and only make use of it, in its own proper place and time, for preaching and disputing when their turn comes, and afterwards give their minds to the simple and naked Contemplation of God, without form, figure or consideration.

181. The Study, which is not ordered for God's glory only, is but a short way to Hell; not through the Study, but the Wind of Pride, which begets it. Miserable is the greatest part of Men at this time, whose only Study is to satisfie the unsatisfiable curiosity of Nature.

182. Many seek God and find him not; because they are more moved by curiosity than sincere, pure and upright intention: they rather desire Spiritual Comforts than God himself; and as they seek him not with truth, they neither find God nor Spiritual Pleasures.

183. He that does not endeavour the total denying of himself, will not be truly abstracted; and so can never be capable of the truth and the light of the Spirit. To go towards the mystical Science, a man must never meddle with things which are without, but with prudence, and in that which his Office calls him to. Rare are men who set a higher price upon hearing than speaking? But the wise and purely mystical Man never speaks but when he cannot help it; nor doth he concern himself in any thing but what belongs to his Office, and then he carries himself with great Prudence.

184. The spirit of Divine Wisdom fills men with Sweetness, governs them with Courage, and enlightens those with excellence who are subject to its direction. Where the Divine Spirit dwells, there is always simplicity and a holy Liberty. But Craft and Double-mindedness, Fiction, Artifices, Policy and worldly Respects, are Hell it self to wise and sincere men.

185. Know that he who would attain to the Mystical Science, must be denied and taken off from five things: 1. From the Creatures. 2. From Temporal things. 3. From the very Gifts of the Holy Ghost. 4. From himself. 5. He must be lost in God. This last is the compleatest of all; because that Soul only that knows how to be so taken off, is that which attains to being lost in God, and only knows where to be in safety.

186. God is more satisfied with the affection of the Heart, than that of Worldly Science. 'Tis one thing to cleanse the Heart of all that which captivates and pollutes it, and another to do a thousand things, though good and holy, without minding that purity of Heart which is the main of all for attaining of Divine Wisdom.

187. Never wilt thou get to this Sovereign and Divine Wisdom, if thou hast not strength, when God cleanseth thee in his own time, not only of thy adherency to Temporal and Natural Blessings, but further, to Supernatural and Sublime ones, such as internal Communications, Extasies, Raptures, and other gratuitous Graces, whereon the Soul rests and entertains it self.

188. Many Souls come short of arriving to quiet Contemplation, to divine Wisdom and true Knowledge, notwithstanding that they spend many Hours in Prayer, and receive the Sacrament every day; because they do not subject and submit themselves wholly and entirely to him that hath Light, nor deny and conquer themselves, nor give up themselves totally to God, with a perfect divesting and disinteresting of themselves: In a word, till the Soul be purified in the Fire of Inward Pain, it will never get to a State of Renovation, of Transformation, of perfect Contemplation, of divine Wisdom and affective Union.

SECTION NINETEEN: *Of True and Perfect Annihilation*

189. Thou must know that all this Fabriek of Annihilation hath its foundation but in two Principles. The first is, to keep ones self and all worldly things in a low esteem and value; from whence the putting in practice of this Self-divesting, and of Self-renunciation and forsaking all created things, must have its rise, and that with the affection, and in deed.

190. The second Principle must be a great esteem of God, to love, adore and follow him without the least interest of ones own, let it be never so holy. From these two Principles will arise a full conformity to the Divine Will. This powerful and practical conformity to the Divine Will in all things, leads the Soul to Annihilation and Transformation with God, without the mixture of Raptures, or external Extasies, or vehement Affections: This way being liable to many illusions, with the danger of weakness and anguish of the understanding, by which path there is seldom any that gets up to the top of perfection, which is acquired by t'other safe, firm and real way, though not without a weighty Cross; because therein the Highway of Annihilation and Perfection is founded; which is seconded by many gifts of Light and divine Effects, and infinite other Graces, *gratis data*, yet the Soul that is annihilated must be uncloathed of it all, if it would not have 'em be a hindrance to it in its way to Deification.

191. As the Soul makes continual progress from its meanness, it ought to walk on to the practice of Annihilation, which consists in the abhorring of Honour, Dignity and Praise; there being no reason that Dignity and Honour should be given to Vileness and a meer Nothing.

192. To the Soul that is sensible of its own Vileness, it appear an impossible thing to deserve any thing; 'tis rather confounded and knows it self unworthy of Vertue and Praise: it embraces with equal courage all

occasions of Contempt, Persecution, Infamy, Shame and Affront; and as truly deserving of such reproaches, it renders the Lord thanks, when it lights upon such occasions, to be treated as it deserves; and knows it self also unworthy, that he should use his Justice upon it; but above all, 'tis glad of contempt and affront, because its God gets great glory by it.

193. Such a Soul as this always chooses the lowest, the vilest, and the most despised degree, as well of place, as of cloathing, and of all other things, without the least affectation of singularity; being of the opinion, that the greatest Vileness is beyond its deserts, and acknowledging it self also unworthy even of this. This is the practice that brings the Soul to a true Annihilation of it self.

114. The Soul that would be perfect, begins to mortifie its Passions; and when 'tis advanced in that Exercise, it denies it self; then with the Divine Aid, it passes to the State of Nothing, where it despises, abhors and plunges it self upon the knowledge that it is nothing, that it can do nothing, and that it is worth nothing. From hence springs the dying in it self, and in its senses, in many ways, and at all hours; and finally, from this spiritual Death the true and perfect Annihilation derives its original; insomuch, that when the Soul is once dead to its will and understanding, 'tis properly said to be arrived at the perfect and happy state of Annihilation, which is the last disposition for Transformation and Union, which the Soul it self doth not understand, because 'twould not be annihilated if it should come to know it. And although it do get to this happy state of Annihilation, yet it must know that it must walk still on, and must be further and further purified and annihilated. [Here is most delicious Nonsense, and a very curious Bull.]

195. You must know, that this Annihilation to make it perfect in the Soul, must be in a man's own Judgment, in his Will, in his Works, Inclinations, Desires, Thoughts, and in it Self: so that the Soul must find it self dead to its Will, Desire, Endeavour, Understanding and Thought; willing, as if it did not will; desiring, as if it did not desire; understanding, as if it did not understand; thinking, as if it did not think, without inclining to any thing, embracing equally Contempts and Honours, Benefits and Corrections. O what a happy Soul is that which is thus dead and annihilated! It lives no longer in it self, because God lives in it: And now it may most truly be said of it, that it is a renewed *Phenix*; because 'tis changed, spiritualized, transformed and deified.

SECTION TWENTY: *In which is shewed how this Nothing is the ready way to obtain Purity of Soul, perfect Contemplation, and the rich Treasure of Peace internal.*

196. The way to attain that high state of a Mind reformed, whereby a man immediately gets to the greatest Good, to our first Original, and to the highest Peace, is his Nothingness: Endeavour, O Soul, to be always buried

in that misery. This Nothing, and this acknowledged Misery, is the means by which the Lord works wonders in thy Soul. Cloath thy self with this Nothing, and with this Misery, and see that this Misery and this Nothing be thy continual Food and Habitation, even to the casting down thy self low therein; and then I assure thee, that thou being in that manner, the Nothing, the Lord will be the Whole in thy Soul.

197. Why, thinkest thou, do infinite Souls hinder the abundant Current of the divine gifts? 'Tis only because they would be doing something, and have a desire to be great: all this is to come away from internal Humility, and from their own Nothing; and therefore they prevent those wonders which that infinite goodness would work in 'em. They betake themselves to the very gifts of the Spirit, and there they stick, that they may come out from the Center of Nothing, and so the whole Work is spoil'd. They seek not God with truth, and therefore they find him not: For know thou must, that there is no finding of Him, but in the undervaluing of our own selves, and in nothing.

198. We seek our selves every time we get out of our Nothing; and therefore we never get to quiet and perfect Contemplation. Creep in as far as ever thou canst into the truth of thy Nothing, and then nothing will disquiet thee: Nay, thou wilt be humble and ashamed, losing openly thy own reputation and esteem.

199. O what a strong Bulwark wilt thou find of that Nothing! Who can ever afflict thee, if once thou dost retire into that Fortress? Because the Soul which is despised by it self, and in its own knowledg is Nothing, is not capable of receiving Grievance or Injury from any Body. The Soul which keeps within its Nothing, is internally silent, lives resign'd in any torment whatsoever, by thinking it less than what it doth deserve: It shuns the suspition of a Neighbour, never looks at other folks faults, but its own is free from abundance of Imperfections, and becomes Commander of great Virtue. Whilst the Soul keeps still and quiet in its nothing, it perfects it, it enriches it, the Lord draws his own Image and Likeness in it, without any thing to hinder it.

200. By the way of *Nothing* thou must come to lose thy self in God (which is the last degree of perfection) and happy wilt thou be, if thou canst so lose thy self; then thou wilt get thy self again, and find thy self most certainly. In this same Shop of *Nothing*, Simplicity is made; interior and infused recollection is possessed, quiet is obtained, and the heart is cleansed from all manner of imperfections. O what a Treasure wilt thou find, if thou shalt once fix thy habitation in *Nothing* and if thou once gettest but I'snugg into the Center of *Nothing*, thou will never concern thy self with any thing that is without (the great ugly large step that so many thousand Souls do stumble at) unless it be as thy Office may call thee to it.

201. If thou dost but get shut up in *Nothing*, (where the blows of

adversity can never come) nothing will vex thee or break thy peace. This is the way of getting to the command of thy self, because perfect and true dominion doth only govern in *Nothing*: with the Helmet of *Nothing* thou will be too hard for strong temptations and the terrible suggestions of the envious enemy. [I defie all the *Quakers* in *England* to match this incomparable piece of Nonsence and Enthusiastick Cant.]

202. Knowing that thou art nothing, that thou canst do nothing, and art worth just nothing, thou wilt quietly embrace passive drynesses, thou wilt endure horrible desolations; thou wilt undergo spiritual martyrdoms and inward torments. By means of this *Nothing* thou must die in thy self, many ways, at all times, and all hours.

203. Who must awaken the Soul out of that sweet and pleasant Sleep, if once it comes to take a Nap in Nothing? This is the way that *David* got a perfect annihilation, without so much as knowing it. *Ad nihilum redactus sum de nescivi*, Psal. 17. Keeping thy self in *Nothing*, thou wilt bar the door against every thing that is not God; thou wilt retire also from thine own self, and walk toward that internal solitude, where the Divine Spouse speaks in the Heart of his Bride, teaching her high and divine Wisdom. Drown thy self in this *Nothing*, and there shalt thou find a holy Sanctuary against any Tempest whatsoever.

204. By this way must thou return to the happy state of Innocence forfeited by our first Parents. By this Gate thou must enter into the happy land of the living, where thou wilt find the greatest Good, the breath of Charity, the beauty of Righteousness, the streight Line of Equity and Justice, and, in sum, every jot and tittle of Perfection. Lastly, do not look at *nothing*, desire *nothing*, will *nothing*, nor endeavour *nothing*, and then in every thing thy Soul will live repos'd, with quiet and enjoyment.

205. This is the way to get purity of Soul, perfect contemplation and peace internal; walk therefore in this safe path, and endeavour to overwhelm thy self in this *Nothing*, endeavour to lose thy self, to sink deep into it, if thou hast a mind to be annihilated, united and transformed.

SECTION TWENTY-ONE: *Of the high Felicity of internal Peace, and the wonderful Effects of it.*

206. The Soul being once annihilated and renewed with perfect nakedness, finds in its superiour part a profound peace, and a sweet rest, which brings it to such a perfect Union of love, that it is joyful all over. And such a Soul as this is already arrived to such a happiness, that it neither wills nor desires any thing but what its Beloved wills; it conforms it self to this Will in all emergencies, as well of comfort as anguish, and rejoyces also in every thing to do the Divine Good Pleasure.

207. There is nothing but what comforts it; nor doth it want any thing,

but what it can well want: To die, is enjoyment to it; and to live, is its joy. It is as contented here upon Earth, as it can be in Paradise; it is as glad under privation, as it can be in possession; in sickness as it can be in health; because it know that this is the will of its Lord. This is its life, this is its glory, its paradise, its peace, its repose, its rest, its consolation and highest happiness.

208. If it were necessary to such a Soul as this, which is gotten up by the steps of annihilation to the region of peace, to make its choice, it would chuse desolation before comfort, contempt before honour; because the loving Jesus made great esteem of reproach and pain: if it first endured the hunger of the blessings of Heaven, if it thirsted for God, if it had the fear of losing him, the lamentation of heart, and the fighting of the Devil; now things are altered, and hunger is turned into satisfying, the thirst into satiety, the fear into assurance, the sadness into joy, the weeping into merriment, and the fierce fighting into the greatest peace. O happy Soul, that enjoys here on earth so great a felicity! Thou must know, that these kind of Souls (though few they are) be the strong Pillars which support the Church, and such as abate the divine indignation.

209. And now this Soul that is entered into the heaven of peace, acknowledges it self full of God and his supernatural gifts, because it lives grounded in a pure love, receiving equal Pleasure in light and darkness, in night and day, in affliction and consolation. Through this holy and heavenly indifference, it never loses its peace in adversity, nor its tranquility in tribulations, but sees it self full of unspeakable enjoyments.

210. And although the Prince of Darkness makes all the assaults of Hell against it, with horrible temptations, yet it makes head against 'em, and stands like a strong Pillar; no more happening to it by 'em, than happens to a high mountain and a deep valley in the time of storm and tempest.

211. The valley is darkned with thick clouds, fierce tempests of hail, thunder, lightning and hail-stones, which looks like the picture of Hell: at the same time the lofty Mountain glitters by the bright beams of the Sun, in quietness and serenity, continuing clear, like heaven, immovable and full of light.

212. The same happens to this blessed soul; the valley of the part below is suffering tribulations, combats, darkness, desolations, torments, martyrdoms and suggestions; and at the same time, on the lofty mountain of the higher part of the Soul, the true Sun casts its beams; it enflames and enlightens it; and so it becomes clear, peaceable, resplendent, quiet, serene, being a meer ocean of joy.

213. So great therefore is the quiet of this pure Soul, which is gotten up the mountain of tranquility, so great is the peace of its spirit, so great the serenity and chearfulness that is within, that a remnant and glimmering of God do rebound even to the outside of it.

214. Because in the throne of quiet are manifest the perfections of spiritual beauty; here the true light of the secret and divine Mysteries of our holy faith, here perfect humility, even to the annihilation of it self, the amplest resignation, chastity, poverty of spirit, the sincerity and innocence of the Dove, external modesty, silence and internal fortitude, liberty and purity of heart; here the forgetfulness of every created thing, even of it self, joyful simplicity, heavenly indifference, continual Prayer, a total nakedness, perfect disinterestedness, a most wise contemplation, a conversation of heaven; and lastly, the most perfect and serene peace within, of which this happy soul may say what the wise man said of wisdom, that all other graces came along in the company with her. *Venerunt mihi omnia bona pariter cum illa.* Wisd. 7. 11.

215. This is the rich and hidden treasure, this is the lost groat of the Gospel; this it the blessed life, the happy life, the true life, and the blessedness here below. O thou lovely greatness that passest the knowledge of the sons of men! O excellent supernatural life, how admirable and unspeakable art thou, for thou art the very draught of blessedness! O how much dost thou raise a soul from earth, which loses in its view all things of the vileness of earth! thou art poor to look upon; but inwardly thou are full of wealth: thou seemest low, but art exceeding high; in a word, thou art that which makest men live a life divine here below. Give me, O Lord, thou greatest goodness, give me a good portion of this heavenly happiness and true peace, that the World, sensual as it is, is neither capable of understanding nor receiving. *Quem mundus non potest accipere.*

SECTION TWENTY-TWO: *A mournful Exclamation and lamentable Moan to God for the Small Company of Souls that arrive at Perfection, the Loving Union and the Divine Transformation.*

216. O Divine Majesty, in whose presence the Pillars of Heaven do quake and tremble! O thou Goodness, more than infinite, in whose love the Seraphins burn! give me leave, O Lord, to lament our blindness and ingratitude. We all live in Mistakes, seeking the foolish world, and forsaking thee, who art our God. We all forsake thee, the Fountain of Living Waters, for the stinking Dirt of the World.

217. O we children of men, how long shall we follow after lying and vanity? Who is it that hath thus deceived us, that we should forsake God our greatest good? Who is it that speaks the most truth to us? Who is it that loves us most? Who defends us most? Who is it that doth more to shew himself a Friend, who more tender to shew himself a Spouse, and more good to be a Father? that our blindness should be so great, that we should all forsake this greatest and infinite goodness?

218. O Divine Lord! what a few Souls are there in the World, which do

serve thee with perfection! how small is the number of those, who are willing to suffer, that they may follow Christ crucified, that they may embrace the Cross, that they may deny and contemn themselves! O what a scarcity of Souls is there, which are disinterested and totally naked! how few are those Souls which are dead to themselves and alive to God, which are totally resigned to his divine good pleasure! How few those, who are adorn'd with simple obedience, profound knowledg of themselves; and true humility! how few those, which with an entire indifference give up themselves into the hands of God, to do what he pleases with 'em! how few are there of those pure Souls which be of a simple and disinterested heart, and which, putting off their own understanding, knowledg, desire and will, do long for self-denial and spiritual death! O what a scarcity of Souls is there which are willing to let the Divine Creator work in 'em a mind to suffer, that they may not suffer, and to die, that they may not die! How few are the Souls which are willing to forget themselves, to free their hearts from their own affections, their own desires, their own satisfactions, their own love and judgments! that are willing to be led by the highway of self-denial and the internal way! that are willing to be annihilated, dying to themselves and their senses! that are willing to let themselves be emptied, purified and uncloathed, that God may fill and cloath and perfect 'em! In a word, how small, O Lord, is the number of those Souls which are blind, deaf and dumb and perfectly contemplative!

219. O the shame of us the Children of *Adam*! who, for a thing of meer vileness, do despise true felicity, and hinder our greatest good, the rich treasure and infinite goodness! Great reason has Heaven to lament, that there are so few Souls to follow its precious path-way. *Viæ Sion lugent, eo quod non sint qui veniant ad solennitatem.* (Lam. 1.4)

I submit every thing, with humble prostration, to the Correction of the Holy Roman Catholick Church.

A Brief Treatise Concerning Daily Communion

by Miguel de Molinos

PREFACE:

The following Treatise was approved of at Rome by Fryer Pater Damian, a Discalceate Carmelite, Visitor General and Reader of Theology in the Convent of S. Mary della Scala, in the Year 1675, when the foregoing Book was so highly applauded and set out with so many Formallities: And after him, Nicholas Martinez, a Jesuite, Chief Reader of Theology in the Roman Colledg, (which is one of the eminentest Offices in one of the most eminent Houses of Education in the whole City) comes to set his Approbation to it: And then, after these two, our old Friend, that we were beholden to before, Fryer Dominick of the most Holy Trinity, Qualifier of the Holy Office in Rome, &c. he tells us, that forasmuch as he found nothing in it contrary to Faith or good Manners, or repugnant to the Reverence due to the Sacrament, &c. he takes it to be worthy to be Printed for divers and sundry reasons. So that though it met not with those Acclamations which the former Book did, (the reason whereof you will presently smell out, when you read it) yet these three Testimonies (besides the pains that the devout Priest (as he calls himself) took to get it out of Spanish into Italian) were enough to give it Credit and Authority in the World: And as it came tack't to t'other Book so 'twas pity to make it part Company.

But whilst these Reverend Gentlemen have been so kind to help it into the World, and speak such good things of it, 'tis plain that they either wink't at, or did not know one gross Contradiction that it makes to the foregoing Book; and that is this: That this, Mich. Molinos does lay it down as a Principle, in his Spiritual Guide, That the Penitent ought to resign up his Will, his Judgment, his Knowledge, his Choice to the determination of his Spiritual Director. And produces Examples for it, and tells him, that he must be led blindfold by his Confessor, though he should put him upon never so useless and nonsensical Penance and Mortification, as planting Lettice with the Roots upwards, &c. (a specimen of which sort of asinine and undisputing Obedience is to be seen pressed by the Founder of the Jesuitical Order, in his Epistle to the Brethren of his Society, Reg. Soc. Jesu, Cap. 18. wherein he instances in Abbot John, that watered a withered Tree for a whole Year together; (Which did him as much good as if he had tied a Whiting to his Girdle.) And, at his Superiour's command, tried to move a vast Stone which was beyond the strength of many men together to do; which he had no more reason to do, than to knock his Head against it). And the reason that is given for this sort of affected and foolish Humility, forsooth, must be because the Father Confessor is in God's place, and whatever he enjoyns his Penitent, must be done by an absolute and unlimited Obedience, without asking, why or wherefore, or entring into any thoughts of the reasonableness or unreasonableness, convenience or inconvenience, good or hurt of such a ranting sort of Discipline: And what fine work may there be sometimes done, when a silly Priest meets with a Penitent that is as wise as himself? But if the business be really, thus, then what's the reason that this Author doth so often in this Treatise, flie in the face of the Ministers, (who in his sense, are these Confessors) and tax them with I know not what, and make most lamentable out-cries against 'em for hindring their Penitents from Daily Communion? This is going backward and forward, saying and unsaying again: For if the Confessor have a power of disposing of his Penitent's (I was going to say Client's) Will, &c. as he pleases, and an unaccountable Empire and Government over him; I would fain see how he can advise him amiss? And why should all this noise be made against these Ministers who are made Judges of the disposition of their People, whom they Shrine, and therefore are presumed to do no more than what there is reason for, in hindring 'em from Daily Communion?

If the foregoing Book were first Penn'd by the Author, then he either retracted his judgment, in this Treatise, or else forgot himself, (which he presses often as a Duty of Religion.) If this Treatise was Penn'd first, then the Author was willing to give Confessors more scope and power in [his Spiritual Guide] than he though fit to allow 'em in his [Daily Communion.] However the matter was, there is a filthy Mistake some where or other; to press blind Obedience to Confessors in one Book, and yet bawl at 'em for requiring it in another. The least that can be said of it, is, that 'tis an argument of an inconstant or forgetful Head, And I leave it to him to make it out, or to any body else that has a mind to clear the point. The Treatise it self is like other Popish Treatises upon that Subject; only 'tis a question, whether the Author be so far Annihilated yet (as his word is) as to believe Transubstantiation so stoutly as others of that Communion would make us believer they do. He hath been mightily conversant in ModernCasuists and Schoolmen, and that makes him so ill a Divine, as to tell us of receiving good by the Sacrament ex opere operato; i.e. Never minding what is done, but only the doing the bare action of it. I could not forbear shewing a mark of dislike, when I found him quoting two such bouncing Authorities out of St. Austine and St. Jerome for delivering Souls out of Purgatory by the efficacy of Mass. I confess they are very pregnant for his purpose, if he can but shew us those Words in the true Writings of those two Fathers: but to send us to the Man in the Moon to know further, this is not fair nor Scholar-like. If any man else will undertake to shew us those Words in the undoubted and unforg'd Works of St. Austine and St. Jerome, he will make me (for my part) in that point..

A Quietist.

THE AUTHOR'S ADVERTISEMENT:

Tis none of my intention to Discourse in this subject by the way of Humane Respect or Passion, nor to defend hard Controversies, nor promote my own Opinions; and though I have Written this short Treatise at the continual ingagements and instances of Zealous Persons, yet God's greater Glory, and the Spiritual advantage of Souls, have been my only desire: Nor is it any less my design, that by this Treatise and these Reasons, the Faithful should govern themselves in the business of frequent Communion, without the Prudent and Holy Counsel of their Spiritual Fathers; because I always look upon it more fitting to obey their Orders, though it should hinder the Communion, than to communicate every day according to their own Sense and Judgment. This Compendium of the Reasons and Authorities of Councils, Saints, and Doctors, is only drawn up a-purpose, that Confessors may see the small reason there is to hinder those Souls from taking the Communion, which desire it, receive good by it, and are obedient to their Directions.

SECTION ONE: *No Minister ought to keep a faithful Person from the Communion, that does desire and ask it, whilst he doth not know his Conscience defiled with mortal Sin.*

The Council of *Trent*, treating of the Preparation which Priests and Layman ought to make for the worthy Receiving of the Holy Eucharist, hath these following words, (*Sess. 13, Cap. 17.*) The Custom of the Church makes it clear, that Examination and Proof is necessary in order to the Communion; that no man, knowing himself guilty of mortal Sin, though he may seem Contrite to himself, come to the Sacrament, unless he have before been at Sacramental Confession. Which comprehends all Christians, and even Priests, who are bound by their Office to Celebrate it: from whence 'tis clearly to be inferred, that the Council makes no other disposition necessary for the Communicating of Laymen, and the Priest's saying Mass, than not to have any mortal Sin. Why then should the Ministers be a hindrance to those which have that disposition?

The Ministers will not say that their Authority is greater than that of the Council; nor that they are more Learned than all those Fathers of the Church that came to it; nor will they say, less, that they have a greater light from God, than that which he then communicated to his Spouse, the Church: Therefore the Ministers ought not to require a greater disposition, than being without mortal Sin, whilst the Council requires no more.

Either the Ministers and Priests, which say Mass daily, have this Holiness and Perfection themselves, which they require in Laymen, or else they have it not: they will not say they have it, because it would then be pride in 'em: If they have it not, and yet Celebrate Mass every day, why do they require it from Laymen, in order to the granting 'em the Communion daily? 'Tis good to advise 'em to this Perfection, but if they should not have it, it will not be reasonable to deprive 'em of so great a good, because they may have reason to fear that Christ our Lord may say to 'em as he did to the *Pharisees*, (St. Matthew 23.24) That they bind heavy burthens upon men, and they themselves will not touch 'em with one of their fingers. And that also is verified which *David* said, (Psalm 61. 10) That men are deceitful in the weight. *Mendaces filii hominum in stateris*; Since they have one weight for themselves and another for Laymen.

If the Council judges that not being in mortal Sin, is a worthy disposition towards saying Mass daily, consecrating and offering Sacrifice, which is the holiest Service, how much more worthy will such a disposition be for only the receiving the Communion?

If Councils, the Church, Popes, Saints, and Doctors tequire no greater disposition to receive fruit from this Sacrament, than not being in mortal Sin, why must the Ministers require a greater?

The Council of Trent hath the following words: (*Sess. 28. Cap. 6.*) *Optaret quidem Sancta Synodus ut in singulis missis fideles adstantes, non solum spirituali affectu, sed Sacramentali etiam Eucharistiæ preceptione Communicarent, quo ad eos hujus sacrificii fructus uberior perveniret.* That is, the holy Council would look upon it as a very good thing that in every days Mass, the Faithful who assist at it, would be Communicated, not only Spiritually and in their desires, but also Sacramentally by receiving the Holy Eucharist, that they might thus obtain the more abundant benefit by this most Holy Sacrament. The Council therefore desires that the Faithful would communicate every day that they hear Mass, with the disposition of having no mortal Sin, as it signified *Sess. 13. chap. 7.* Will any Ministers say, that this is not well, and so openly set themselves in opposition to the desires of the Church?

The Congregation of the Council declared it an Errour that any Bishops in a Capriccio should limit and hinder Daily Communion from being taken by Merchants and House-keepers: The holy *Rota* reports it in the year 1587 (*Barbos. in Council. Trid. Sup. c. 22.*) and after it had Decreed that all Laymen might be communicated, even every day, though they should be Merchants and House-keepers, it adds the following words: — *Qua propter exhortandi sunt fideles, ut sicut quotidie peccant, ita quotidie medicinam accipient:* That is, wherefore the Faithful are to be exohorted, that as they Sin daily, so they daily receive this Medicine of the Sacrament of the Eucharist. And the same Coucil of *Trent* says. (*Sess. 13. c. 2. de Instit. Sanctiss. Sacr.*) *Qui manducat me, ipse vivet propter me, & tanquam antidotum, quo liberemur a culpis quotidianis & a peccatis mortalibus præfervemur:* ---- The Communion is as an Antidote to free us from daily Sins, and preserve us from mortal Sins. If the Council and its Decree speaks here, not of the *Basils* and *Antonies*, nor of the *Catharines* and *Clares*, as some say it is required for 'em to be, but of those that Sin daily; why should they be kept from the Medicine, that they may not Sin?

The Council of *Milan* (*3 de Euch.*) and that of *Cabilon* (*Cant. 46.*) are of the same mind.

The blessed Pius Quintus says, (*Catech. Rom. 2. p. c. 4. §. 60.*) The Curates are bound to exhort the Faithful often, that as they hold it necessary to feed the Body daily, so they hold it also necessary to feed the Soul as often with this Sacrament: because the Children of *Israel* did eat *Manna* in the wilderness daily; and that *Manna* was the Figure of this sacred Food; And that sentence [Thou sinnest every day, be communicated also every day.] is not only St. Augustine's, but the saying of all the Saints.

St. Ignatius, Bishop and Martyr, (*Epist. ad Eph.*) exhorts that we often come and receive the Eucharist; because the frequency of it weakens the power of Satan. The Council of *Alexandria* says, (*De Euch.c. 5.*) That without this frequency, it will be a hard matter to preserve Grace. St. John Chrisostome (*In Epist. S. Paul ad Tim.*) says, It is no rashness for a Christian to come often to the Sacrament: he that remembers not a great fault of himself, may come to it every day.

Theophylact (*In Prim. S. Paul ad Corinth. II.*) says, To know whether thou mayest Communicate, be thou the Judge, and having examined thy self, thou mayest do it, without staying for a Festival., unless thou findest thy self burthened with a great fault.

St. Cyprian (*In Orat. Dom. Serm. 6.*) says, Let us ask this daily Bread, being in no great fault let us receive this Bread every day, which gives us

Life Eternal; and let us beg that our Bread, which is Christ our Lord, may be daily given us, to keep us in his Grace: No small loss it is, to forbear Communicating every day.

St. Hilary says, (*De Consectrat. dist. 2. cap. 51.*) If thy Sins are not so greivous as to deserve Excommunication, not being mortal, if they should be mortal, after Confession, as Suarez expounds it, *Disp. 60.Sess. 3*) never keep off from the daily Medicine, which is the Body and Blood of the Lord.

St. Ambrose says, (*5 de Sacram. c. 4.*) Receive daily, that which is to help thee daily: he that does not deserve to receive it every day, doth not deserve to receive it in a whole year: Sins are daily committed, and therefore this Divine Bread is for every day. Thou offendest every day, wash thy self therefore of thy Sin every day in the Fountain of Repentance; and if thou comest every day to this Divine Sacrament, thou wilt find wholesome Medicine, and not the Poison of Judgment.

St. Jerom says, (*In Apol. Cont. Jovin.*) We should always receive the Holy Eucharist, that we may be without mortal Sin: And in his time, which was the Year 470, he says, the holy Custom of Communicating every day, continued in *Rome* and in *Spain.*

St. Augustine says, (*Tract. 26. in Johan.*) If thou comest without Sin, come and welcome; 'tis Bread and not Poyson;

Again, (*Ep. de ver. Dom. Ser. 28.*) 'Tis better to Communicate for Devotion, than let it alone for Reverence. And in another place, This is the daily Bread, receive it daily, because it will daily do thee good, and thou mayest receive it every day.

Some ascribe that sentence to the same Father, *Quotidie Eucharistiæ Communionem percipere, nec laudo nec reprehendo.* With which a Bishop reproved S. Catharine of Siena, because she took the Sacrament every day: and the Saint replied to him, how he durst reprove in her, that which St. Austine durst not reprove? Bellarmine therefore (*De Script. Eccles. in the Year 420.*) says that this sentence is not S. Austine's, but Gennadius's of Marseilles; and so many other Authors assure us.

S. Gregory (*De Confeor d. 2. c. Quid sit Sanguis.*) says, The Lord gave us this Salutary Sacrament to pardon our daily sins; let us receive it every day.

St. Bernard (*In Serm. de Cæna Dom.*) says, The wounded man seeks Medicine: we are all of us wounded, when we have Sinned; our Medicine is the Divine Sacrament: receive it daily and thou wilt recover daily.

St. Apollonius (*In vitis Patrum ejus vita.*) advised his Monks to be communicated every day, that they might be preserved in Grace.

St. Bonaventure, (*De Præcept. Relig. Proces. 7. c. 21.*) Though thou shouldst find thy self lukewarm, with little Fervour in thee, yet trusting in the Mercy of God, thou mayst safely come to the Communion: if thou think'st thy self unworthy, (so that thou remembrest no mortal Sin of thine own) come; because the weaker thou art, the greater need hast thou of the Physitian.

Thou do'st not receive Christ to sanctify Him, but that he may sanctify thee.

The Council of *Alexandria* (*Cap. 5. de Euchar.*) says, Without this frequency, 'tis hard to keep in Grace.

S. Antony of Florence (*Par. 3. lib. 14. cap. 12. § 5. & 6.*) says, Those that live well must be sure to be advised to receive this most holy Sacrament frequently; because as long abstinence from bodily Food, weakens the Body, and disposes it for Death, so the much abstaining from this spiritual Food, weakens the Soul, spends the fervour, and by degrees inclines it to mortal Sin.

Pope Adrian (*In 4 Sent. Tract. de Euchar.*) says, When once the preparation is made according to Humane frailty, 'tis safer to receive than keep from the most Holy Sacrament.

St. Thomas Aquinas (*3 Par. quæst. 80. art. 10.*) asks, If it be lawful to Communicate every day? And answers with St. *Austine*, This is daily Bread: receive it every day, that thou mayest every day be profited by it.

St. Isidore (*Lib. 3. de Eccles. Offic.*) hath this, Some say, that if there be no Sin, the Communion ought to be taken daily; and they say well, if they receive it with Veneration and Humility.

St. Anaclete, Pope, (*De Conscer. dist. 1 & 2. ca. Peracta.*) perceiving Daily Communion grow into disuse, brought it up again, ordering, that after Consecration all those that were present should be communicated, because this Custom (as he says in a Decree of his) was established by the Apostles and kept hy the *Roman* Church: and those that did not communicate, were turn'd out of the Church.

Innocent the Third (*in tract. Miss. lib. 4. cap. 44.*) says, He may communicate who has his conscience free from mortal sin, and is grieved for that which is venial.

St. Athanasius, (*1 ad Cor. probit autem*) having examined thy Conscience, always come to the Communion, without staying for a holy day.

Henriquez relates it, (*lib. 8. de Euchar. cap. 88. n. 2.*) that St. Austin, St. Ambrose, and St. Jerome, do commend those who communicate daily, without fail. Those that the Confessor shall judge worthy of absolution, may be advised by him to receive the Communion, though they fear an easie relapse. 'Tis not necessary to make an experiment of frequent Communion from a man's good and profit by it: because spiritual profit (which is insensible) is much less found than corporal profit.

Thomas a Kempis (*lib. 4. de imit. Christi*) says, If I am luke-warm when I do communicate, what should I be, if I should not communicate? I would add, if I am naughty when I do communicate, by not communicating I should offend the whole world and damn my self.

The following Doctors defend Daily Communion with very strong reasons, which for brevity sake are omitted.

Innocent the Third, *tract. de Missa, lib. 4. cap. 44.*

St. Athanasius, *I Cor. II. probit autem*

Heneriquez, *lib. 8. de Euchar. c. 88. n. 2.*

Thomas a Kempis, *lib. 4. de imit. Christi, cap. 3.*

Alexander of Hales, *4 part. quæst. 51. art. 10.*

Gerson, *in opere tripart. cap 19.*

The Patriach of Jerusalem, *in 4. dist. 12. quæst. 2.*

John Colaya, *in 4. sent dist. 12. q. 2*

Ranier of Pisa, *I part.tract. Euchar. cap. 26.*

Martin of Ledesma, *p. I. q. 4. art 10.*

Nider, *in præcept. 3. cap. 12. n. 12.*

Astensis, *in sum. 2. par. lib. 4. tit. 27.*

Father Salmeron, *tom. 9. tract. 41.*

Father Francis Suarez, *tom. 3. disp. 63. sect. 3.*

Durandin 4, *dist. 12. qu. 5.*

Victoria, *in Sum. quæst.*

John of Friburg, *sum lib. 3. de Euchar. tit. 24.*

John Altestaing, *lib. 4. cap. 5.*

Gabriel Mayor, *in sum.tract. 3. de Euch.*

Raimond, *in sum. tract. 3. de Euchar.*

Peter de Soto, *in 4 dist. 22. qu. I. art. 10.*

Lewis Blois, *dialog. Suson.*

Stephen Boluser, *lib. 4. dist. 12. qu. 14.*

Rosela, *sum. tract. 3. de Euchar.*

Father Christopher of Madrid, *de frequent. Commun. cap. I.*

Reynalds, *de prudent. Conf. c. I I.*

Francis de Lavata, *verb. Euchar. propof. 18.*

Dionysius Carthusianus, *de Euch. cap. 5.*

John Mayor, *in 4 dist. 9. qu. 1.*

Venantius Fortunatus, *in Orat. Dominic.*

Cardinal Hosias, *de Cerem. sol. 371*

Bishop Perez, *de Sacram. qu. 80. ar. 9.*

Vivaldus, *de Euch, n. 139.*

Christopher Morenus, *lib. Claredad de simples.*

James Baius, *de instit. relig. Christ. lib. 2. cap. 19.*

The illumniate Father John Thaulerus, *Serm. I. Dom. 7 post Trin.*

Alphonse Rodriguez, *2. p. treat. 8. cap. 10.*

Antony Molina, *tract. 7. pag. 870*

Lewis Fandone, *tract. de divin. Sacram. p. 2. cap. II.*

Father Joseph of St. Mary, *tract. de Com.*

Raimund Sebunde, *dial 7. cap. 17.*

Mauras Antonius, *de Euch. cap. 5.*

Peter Marsilia, *Memor. Compost. fol. 62.*

Father Antony de Alvarado, *in his Guide of Slaves, fol. 414.*

Alphonse of Chinchilla, *tract. Commun. document. 3.*

Father Lewis of Granada, *tract. 3. cap. 8. sect. 2.*

Villalobos, *I part. tract. 3. dif. 4. n. 3.*

Almai, *in 4 dist. 26.*

John Sanchez, *dist. 23. n. 13*

Palao, *in 4 dist. 31. disc. 2.*

Basil, *lib. I Matrim. cap. 12. n. 6.*

Veracruz, *3. par. spec. art. 16.*

Sa. de verb, *Euchar. n. 12*

Henry Henriquez, *in sum. lib. 8 de Euchar. cap. 48*

Ferrer, *Art of knowing Jesus, 3 part. dial. 5.*

Escobar, *lib. 2. sess. 4. de notat. san.*

Mendoza, *par. 3. tract. de Sacr. instr. 32.*

Cassian, *in Vitis Patrum.*

Medini, *lib. I. cap. 14.*

Jerom Perez, *in sum. Theolog.*

Adrian, *in 4 sent. tract. de Euchar.*

Finally, the illuminate Thauler says, that to receive the most holy Sacrament without mortal sin, as has been said, does more good than to hear a hundred Masses, or a hundred Sermons: and so say many Authors, as Jerom Perez relates (*insum. Theolog. de Euch.*) that he does but once receive the most holy Sacrament without mortal sin, gets more grace by it, than if he should go thrice in Pilgrimage to the holy Sepulcher at *Jerusalem;* and that never did any body communicate, without obtaining particular Grace thereby, and a singular degree of Charity which he had not before, though he were never so lukewarm and dry.

A grave religious man adds this consideration, That if all the Charity should be put together, which all man have had or shall have, which have been, are, or shall be, and the merits of 'em all, and the praises that have been given and shall be given, and all the good works which have been done and shall be done, and the torments of Martyrs, the Fastings, Disciplines, and Hair-cloaths of all the Saints, Confessors, Patriarchs, Virgins and Prophets, with whatever else that shall be done as long as the World indures; put it all together, and it doth not please God so much, as the receiving of this Divine Sacrament.

Others say, as the abovesaid Author relates, that if all the Quires of Angels, all the Courtiers of Heaven, and the most holy Virgin (Mistress of 'em all, who incomparably exceed 'em all) should meet together, it is not in their power to do a more pleasing Sacrifice to God, nor a more acceptable Offering, than Saying of Mass, or, when men communicate, to offer to his Majesty that Divine Sacrament.

St. Cyril (in *S. Johan, c. 37. & lib. 4. c. 17.*) affirms, that the only delaying of it never creates a better disposition to it; and it commonly happens, that those who are slowest to come to the Communion, come less prepared: and further, these following Reasons do make it evident. To communicate worthily without mortal sin is good of it self; to forbear it, is not so: To go often to the Sacrament is a product of Charity: to delay it, comes from negligence or fear: better is the work of Charity than that of Fear. He that communicates gets the better of him that lets it alone in the good he receives by the Sacrament *Ex opere operato*: and at the most may easily be equal to him, since the desire of communicating worthily, is no less good, than keeping from it out of reverence. If it be sometimes good to abstain, it ought to be for the obtaining or preserving the reverence and devotion of it: and for this reason the frequency of the most holy Sacrament is not of less advantage, since thereby the Soul gets cleansed of those evil habits and affections and natural imperfections that we have.

If the Scripture therefore in many places, if the Apostles, Councils, Popes, and the Saints and Doctors do advise us to daily communion, without limitation or laxing, and if there be no Law divine or humane to forbid it to him that has no mortal sin to hinder him, what is the reason that the Ministers should forbid or limit that which neither Christ nor the Church nor any Law does limit? 'Twill be prudence therefore not to oppose the Sayings of Doctors, Saints, Popes and Councils, to get free from the punishment given to many Ministers for forbidding of it.

Father Bernadino of Villagas, in the *Life of St. Lutgard, chap. 25.* says, that among other persons that thought ill of the frequent communion of that Saint, the Abbess was one, who being led by an indiscreet zeal, ordered her not to communicate so often: to whom the humble Virgin returned this Answer, with great reverence, That she was ready and prepared to obey her order with content, but she knew for certain, that this disfavour she did her, would displease Jesus Christ, and that in the punishment which would follow, she would quickly understand how ill she did, in depriving her of the Communion. The Saint obeyed, and in recompence of her obedience, it seems, the Lord making good the Voice of her Prophecy, sent the Abbess a great fit of sickness, which afflicted her much with continual and sharp pains, till acknowledging her fault, and that this chastisement befel her for her indiscreet zeal used to the Saint, she sent for her and gave her leave to follow her holy custom, and so the fault ending, the punishment ended also, and the disease which had brought her to a very sad condition. Other persons also who in like manner used to keep a pother with the Saint about her often Communions, repenting of what they had done, askt her pardon. And other of their complices in their prate and gossippings, because they never laid to heart what they had said of her, were punished of God with a sudden death.

In the *third Book of St. Gertrudes Life chap. 23.* 'tis told, that a certain

Preacher or Confessor, being a little warm'd with the zeal of God's Honour, took a pet at some religious Women, thinking that they were often communicated: At this the Saint made a Prayer, and askt the Lord, Whether this were acceptable to him, or no? The Lord make her this answer; it being my delight to be with the children of men, and I having, of infinite love, left this Sacrament to be often received in remembrance of me, and being in it to the faithful to the World's end, whosoever shall, with words or other ways of perswasion, to go about to hinder any from taking it, who are free from mortal sin, doth in a certain manner hinder me, and rob me of my pleasure and delight, which I might have with 'em. Some Ministers there are who have had a mind to restrain this matter too much: as if the Sacrament were not instituted for Laymen, or as if they had no right to ask it as often as they are disposed to receive it. O, as if Christ our Lord had instituted it with a limitation or precept, that is should not be taken but by such and such men, and on such and such days.

Expert Teachers do strangely wonder to see the scruple and cautiousness, with which some Confessors speak about this matter, as if the Communion were a very dangerous thing for Souls, or through the too much frequenting of it, the Honour of God or the Vertue of the Sacraments must need be lost or lessened: whereas the frequency of it is the very remedy and health of Souls and the work in which there is the greatest honour done to God and which they ought most to endeavour, who desire his glory.

And if the Minister should at any time find himself dissatisfied at this, let him peruse that holy Appointment of the Church, (*De Consecr. dist. 2. Aug. in Ps. 48.*) *Non prohibeat dispensator manducare pingues terra in mensa Domini.* And if the dispenser himself cannot hinder this, much less can they hinder it, who have nothing to do to dispense it: and if this which has been said is not enough, let him be afraid of those infinite Punishments which God has rised upon those Ministers which have forbid it.

But for all this, the Communion should always be used at the spiritual Father's order, who neither ought to hinder nor delay it, when he knows the Soul, that desires it and reaps good of it, to be so disposed as the Council requires. And if another Confessor should order him the quite contrary, let him follow the judgment of that ghostly Father, who knows better than any other, how his Conscience is, and by whose Counsel he goes and acts safely.

SECTION TWO: *Answering the Reasons which those Ministers give, which hinder the Faithful from Communicating, and the Priest from Celebrating, having their Consciences free from Mortal Sin.*

Either the Communion must be forbidden to those that ask it and desire it without the guilt of Mortal Sin, because they are not worthy of it, or for the greater reverence of it, or, because much Familiarity breeds Contempt, or else for Mortification and Penance: The first reason, of not being worthy, is not sufficient; because if they make a Christian forbear, till he be worthy of the Communion, then he must never receive it: because no man is worthy to receive Christ, no not Heaven it self. Whereupon many holy men say, that the Communion taken to day is a disposition for that to morrow.

Besides, that Councils, the Saints and Doctors do assure us, that not being in Mortal sin, is that necessary worthiness and disposition which is required for the Communion; we are not to go to it, as worthy, but as having need of it: we do not go to sanctifie Jesus Christ, but to be sanctified and healed by him, by the means of the Sacrament, as St. Ambrose tells us, -- *I who do continually sin, ought continually to receive the Medicine of this Sacrament against the pestilent Disease of Sin. (Ep 208.)*

Nor may a Christian be debarr'd the Communion for the second reason of greater reverence, because 'tis contrary to St. Austin's Doctrine, who says, (*Ep. 26. de verb. Dom. Serm. 28.*) that 'tis better to communicate through Devotion, than let it alone through Reverence. Dionysius Carthusianus says the same thing, 'Tis better to communicate through Love, than abstain from it through Humility and Fear, (*De Euch. cap. 5. sect. 6.*) There is not more devotion, love and respect shewed to God by less frequent coming to the Sacrament: but rather he loves and fears God most, who without mortal sin, and with a desire of his own spiritual advantage, comes every day to it: and the delaying of it is not a greater disposedness nor veneration, but a manifest temptation.

By keeping away, they think to find better devotion and fervour, and in the mean time they are dry, luke-warm and cold, as we see by experience. These people that will not communicate unless they be sensibly and actually devout, are like those who are cold, who will not come near the fire, till they are warm; or like those sick men that will not ask the Physicians counsel, till they are grown well. Christ's Body is like a spiritual fire, let us approach towards it, and it will warm us. The flesh of Christ, says Damascene, is a live coal, which heats and burns.

The third reason which some give for the hindring Christians the Communion, that desire and ask it, is a certain whimsey or *capricio*, which they imprint in their minds, telling 'em, that to go frequently to the Sacrament is too much familiarity, and that this breeds contempt, *Nimia familiaritas parit contemptum.* O hurtful Deceit! O pernicious Doctrine! though, taught by the Ministers with no bad zeal. Is it possible, that among so many Saints and Doctors of the Church which have written professedly upon this Point, as is manifest by the former Chapter, none of 'em should light upon the reason, that these Ministers talk of? 'Tis well inferred therefore, that 'tis of small consideration and account.

True it is, that to much familiarity is sometimes the occasion of contempt, but of what, and to whom? The too much familiarity with a vile thing, occasions contempt, but how can familiar conversation with a thing that is grave, good, and amiable, how can this cause contempt? In earthly things familiarity begets contempt; because the more one man gets acquainted and intimate with another, he discovers his defects by degrees, and so values him less then he did at first. But with God the thing is quite otherwise: because as the creature proceeds in the knowledge of that fountain of true perfection, by the same measure the love and esteem of that great Lord grows more.

If by communicating daily there could be any defect discovered in Jesus Christ, certain it is, that this frequency and familiarity would breed contempt of him; but the more that boundless ocean of perfection is received, the more is his goodness known, and the greater doth the love, the respect and the reverence to him grow. And if it were true, that to much frequency occasioned contempt, it would be necessary to give laws to God himself, and take care not to render himself so easie and familiar to the Saints and Angels of Heaven, with whom he hath so great and continual an intimacy. Who is more familiar with God than he Angels who continually behold his divine countenance? and what, doth this make 'em leave off honouring, reverencing and loving him?

But they will say, it is not good to abuse this familiarity and intimacy with God. What a blindness is this! what should the meaning of this be, unless they would not have us so united with God, and have a mind that we should serve him at a distance, and not near and more by name than affection. These words arise rather from the little will they have that we should receive this divine Lord, than from the respect of not displeasing him: if they had true charity, and did but heartily love Jesus Christ, they would despise all fear, and not remove us from the frequency of this divine Sacrament; nay, they would desire and prompt us on to receive him daily, that we might be united unto God.

If they know, that Christ desires to be united with us, why should they be unwilling that we should be united with him our great Lord, fearing where no fear is? if they see that an infinite God desires our familiarity and friendship, what is it that they build upon, to hinder us from being his friends? do they think that by this continual frequency that will be tedious to us, without which every thing else is tedious? do they believe that that will make our life uneasie, which gives us life? that that good will be a trouble to us, from which all goodness proceeds? and in a word, that he who is the pleasure and delight of all Creatures, of all the Seraphims, of all the Saints, and of the whole Court of Heaven, will be a tediousness to us? true it is, that he satiates, but never becomes tedious.

Nor any less ought a Christian to be denied the Communion, to mortifie him, which is the fourth reason: because in Mortification, to be without the Communion, he only exercises one Vertue, and in the Communion he exercises 'em all. Would it therefore be well that a Christian, for obtaining one Vertue, should be deprived of all the rest? 'Tis great pity to deprive him of the great good he receives in the Communion, only for mortification-sake: which being well thought of, will prove rather a privation of good than the vertue of mortification.

Besides, to be able to say Mass and communicate perfectly, it is not the best way to leave off communicating and celebrating: but rather 'tis the best that can be, to say Mass and communicate every day, though it be with some imperfections. To inable a man to pray perfectly, or to obtain some vertue in perfection, 'tis not a good way to leave off doing acts of that vertue. Who will say, that to make a perfect Prayer, 'tis a good way to let it alone some days? and that to have patience, 'tis a good way not to do any acts of it? rather the best means to obtain patience and to make a perfect Prayer, is to exercise those things day by day, though there should be some imperfection in 'em.

If the divine Majesty vouchsafes to be with sinners, to lodge in their houses, to eat with 'em at the same Table, (for which he bears for his Arms and commands to be fixed on the doors of his house an Inscription, that says, *This Lord receives sinners and eats at one Table with 'em*) why is the Minister and Servant of this same Lord so loath to receive a Christian, if he be changed and mended by repentance? is it therefore reason that the Ministers of this Lord should limit a thing not limited by their Master?

The Lord invitesus, and calls us to his banquet: and will the servant pretend to give leave to those who are invited, when they are introduced to God in his own house? Let 'em come in, if they have no mortal sin about 'em: and if they have, 'tis washed away in the fountain of repentance. Put this on the account of their Lord, that will have it so, and commands it, though it seem inconvenient to the Minister, wherefore the Lord may answer him with great reason, "'Tis well known, that the sinner costs the nothing, and that having so narrow a breast as thou hast, thou admittest him not to the Communion, though he desires it and I invite him to it: but I came down from Heaven for him, and was made man, suffering 33 years incredible torments, even to death it self. I will have him, thus penitent as he is, and because I am God, I have a heart of infinite extend, where all, how wicked soever they may have been, do come, if they turn to me and become reform'd by means of repentance."

Christ our Lord moves the tongue of Angels to exhort men to frequent Communion, and the Prince of darkness moves the tongues of men to perswade 'em the contrary. The Angel said to *Elijah*, (1 Kings 19. 7.) *Arise and eat, for thou hast a long journey to go.* So the Angel perswades him to the Communion; and not only once, but twice he awaked the Prophet that was asleep, to eat Bread, the figure of the Eucharist. 'Tis the propriety of Angels to invite to frequent Communion. Well did St. Jerom say, ---*He is an Angel to thee who puts thee upon the Communion, and a Devil that hinders thee from it.*

'Tis plain, that the Devil shews himself against this Sacrament more than any other, in that he seeks by so many disturbances and ways to hinder it, amongst which 'tis not the least powerful and effectual which he makes use of by Preachers and Confessors, and Ministers themselves, because many of 'em with a cloak of zeal disturb it. Those who reckon themselves Ministers of Jesus Christ, ought to make it their proper work and business to set themselves against the Devil's intentions; not depriving people of their Daily Communion, but advising 'em to it, and procuring it for 'em.

Fryer Joseph of St. Mary, after he had told us the words of the holy Council of *Trent*, where he says --- that he desires that all men would communicate daily (in his *Apology for frequent Communion*) has these following words --- Is it therefore possible, O my Christian Fathers and Brethren, that the Church should have any such children who do so openly contradict her; and that, understanding from their Mother, that it would be a good thing for Christians to communicate every day, they should say it is not convenient, and so oppose themselves to her and contradict her? Certainly this looks like the Devil's temptation, to hinder the growth of Souls, though it be done with good zeal, and to such as be zealous of God's honour, and of the Church their Mother, this will not look well --- Thus far the Author.

Now let any Summist and Learned Man, that has a great opinion of himself, see whether it be lawful to oppose the Authority of so great a Tribunal and the laudable Custom of the Church and her Declarations, against the Practice and Doctrine of the Apostles, and against the Preaching of the holy Doctors of the Church.

Let not man mutter or deny the holy Communion, (says Lewis Fundone, *tract. de diu. Sacr. p. 2. c. 21. fol. 149.*) as if there were no occasion for it, and let him have a care that God do not deny him Heaven; since to condemn this, is to condemn the commendable Customs and most ancient Practice of the Church and the greatest Servants of God. -- Thus far the Author.

Father Peter of Marselles, a *Benedictine, (addit. ad memor. Compostel. fol. 62.)* says, "That as often as a man communicates without the guilt of mortal sin, either by not having committed it, or by being pardoned it, he receives grace by it. This disposition is not of so small moment, as some think, since the holy Councel of *Trent* thinks it enough for reverence and holiness. They are mightily to be commended, that do their best to perswade the faithful to communicate daily; and consequently, what a great error and prejudice of Soul are they that hinder Lay-men the Sacramental Communion every day.

Nothing but Mortal sin (says St. Thomas) can keep a Christian from the Communion. How therefore does it come to pass, that the Ministers keep men from it, when they have no Mortal sin to indispose 'em.

It would be well considered that Christ is in this Sacrament for salve for our wounds, for comfort to our troubles, and for strength in our adversities, and lastly for a pledge and memorial of the love that he bears to Souls, and that this great Lord stands crying out whether there be any that would have him, and the Souls answer that they will have him, but asking the Ministers of the Church to give 'em their Lord, and divide to them their daily bread, the Ministers turn the deaf ear to it, being stewards for Gods house, and are very pinching and niggardly in distributing that which the Lord commands, and so freely gives.

Such a stinginess as this is to be lamented with Tears of Blood. Who would not weep to see that when Gods hand is so open in giving, his servants should be so close-fisted and covetous in distributing: and that God being so bountiful of his own blessings which cost him his blood, they should be so greedy in a thing that cost 'em nothing? and in a word, this Sacrament being that open fountain of *David*, free to all the Sons of *Jacob*, who go to it for the precious water without giving any thing for it, the Ministers sell it so dear that it costs many even tears of blood to obtain it: which gives 'em the lamentation of *Jeremy*, that they are fain to buy the water which is their own, as dear as if it did belong to some body else.

Master John d' Avila, a Man known sufficiently for his exemplar Goodness and Learning and Preaching, being asked whether a Superiour or one that had the cure of Souls, might deny the Communion to him that should ask it of him every day, not having lawful impediment, made answer thus, My opinion is, that no lawful impediment appearing, the Prelate (and he that in his room hath the business of Administrating the Eucharist) is obliged to give it to him that is under him, every time that he asks it. He that denies the most holy Sacrament, is unjust, and deprives him of his right and due that asks it. A Christian (as S. Thomas says) has so much a right to ask it, that the Prelate cannot deny it him, except if be for a publick sin. Asking it in publick he ought to give it him, though he knows that he has Sin in secret: and then how much more ought he to one that asks it devoutly? he is cruel, he takes away the Spiritual Bread from his Child, and I must condemn him for a sinner in it. All this says the above mentioned Author (in his *Treat. 23. Part 3.*)

Will they say, if it be a good and holy thing to Communicate every day, why doth not the Church then command it? and why did not the Founders of Religions, who were indued with so much light, leave it for a rule? and why did not some Saints imbrace this frequency? Saint Mark the Evangelist cut off his Thumb, that they might not make him ordain. Saint Francis of Assise would never be a Priest. Saint Benet was a long time without Communicating. Before I come to answer, I will ask whether be well, that a man in health should not eat something every day, because the Law doth not command it? why have some Saints abstained from food some days? whether single life be good and not Marriage, as S. Paul says, (I Cor. 7.) because the Law commands it not? and why some Saints have not been Married? whether it be a good and holy thing to hear Mass daily, because the Church does not command it? and why some Saints have retired into the desert, where they could not hear it?

Again, before I come to answer, I will suppose that some examples of the Saints are more to be admired than imitated, and that therefore they do not make a general rule; that if some have not Communicated, they were only a few; and they that did Communicate, numberless: and therefore 'twill be more safe to follow the most and not the fewest. I answer the difficulty and the question; that things necessary ought to be commanded, that which is evil ought to be prohibited, and that which is good and holy ought to be advised. The holy Church doth always act rightly, and therefore she doth not command the faithful to Communicate daily: because how holy and good a thing soever it be, yet 'tis not essentially necessary: and the precept of the Church, always looks at the benefit of the faithful, and so great is our luke-warmness, and the frailty of our times, that a precept of Daily Communion would be an occasion of sin and ruine, and therefore the Church does not injoyn Christians by precept any more than one Communion in a year, though the desires that through devotion men would Communicate every day.

Many men shift off their coming daily to this Divine Banquet, that they may not be taken notice of for it, and that they may give no occasion to others to grumble: and the Ministers hearing this reason, hold their tongues and rest satisfied. O hurtful silence! must they permit, for worldly respects, that the faithful should lose so great a benefit? Is it possible that they should let 'em live at a distance, and separate from God and his sweet and loving friendship, because the world should not censure 'em? if there should be any great account made of what the world says, not only the soul would be lost, but also the judgment. Is it not known, that the world makes it its business to speak ill of what good is, and to persecute those that do not take part with it?

All those that serve great men, do make open shew of the degree of their office, greatness and dignity; and shall a Christian think it a shame to himself to communicate, and be seen in the service of Jesus Christ? If it were an evil work to Communicate every day, it might breed scandal; but if it be the best work that a Christian can do, why should he keep from it through an idle fear of offending his neighbour? The Jews were offended at the good works of Jesus Christ, but for all that, his Majesty never left off doing 'em. He that doth ill and interprets the good that others do in an evil sense, 'tis he that gives cause for the scandal: but to do well, was never a scandal, much less can so great good, as Communicating be one. If a man should take offence by seeing us eat, surely we would not for all that be such fools as to starve our selves.

We ought to take great heed of following vanities and wordly pleasures, that we many not by them offend or scandalize our Neighbour: from these vices we ought to keep our selves, not from Daily Communion, because this cannot cause scandal, but will rather edifie our Neighbour, and by our good example, it may be, he may come to change his life and resolve himself to frequent the Sacraments. O how many people are there that are cheated by these wordly respects! O unhappy men! they are not ashamed to be base in their lives, and yet they are ashamed to be Christians and to be known for such!

SECTION THREE: *Wherein are shewn some of the great benefits, of of which a faithful man is deprived, by being prohibited the Communion, when he is sufficiently disposed for it.*

That the Minister may see and take good notice of the hurt which he does, by depriving the faithful of the Communion, that desire and ask it without the guilt of Mortal Sin, it will be necessary to lay before him some of those infinite benefits of which he defrauds 'em, only in one Communion, that he may undeceive himself that deprives 'em of infinite good for mortification sake.

First he deprives such a one of the increase of grace and glory which he receives in the Communion, whose effect is infallible, *ex opere operato*, though he should have venial sins about him. He also deprives him of the mortification of all his five senses and powers, which he therein performs, whilst his Eyes, his Smelling, his Tast, his Touch, his Imagination, his Understanding and all his knowledge and capacity do tell him that that Host is Bread: by all this he is humbled, mortified, and subdued, whilst he belies that it is not that which he feels and tasts, but that his God and Lord is in it. He deprives him also, by taking the Communion from him, of the cleansing of his sins and evil habits, and being preserved from 'em for the time to come; of many helps which are therein administered to him for the performance of every good thing, and avoiding every evil one? and it may happen that the Eternal Salvation of Damnation of a Soul may depend upon one of these helps. He deprives him of the lessening the pains of Purgatory, which is participated in every Communion. He deprives him of the highest acts of Faith, Hope and Charity, which he exercises, by believing that he receives that God, who he sees not, nor feels, and hoping in him, whom he had not seen and being united with him by love.

God is goodness it self, and he is willing to be communicated through love to Souls, by means of the Divine and Sacramental Bread: Is there a greater happiness in the world? can there be a greater felicity? and shall there be any Minister to deprive the Soul of this benefit? In this wonderful Sacrament Christ is united to the Soul, and becomes one and the same thing with it. *In me manet & ego in illo* (St. John 5.) which fineness of love is the most profound, admirable and worthy of consideration and gratitude, because there is not more to give nor to receive: and what Minister shall deprive the soul of this boundless grace?

All Blessings do here meet together in this precious Food, here all desires of God are fulfilled, here is the loving and sacramental Union, here's the Peace, the Conformity, the Transformation of God, with the Soul, and the Soul with God. By receiving Jesus in this Sacrament, the Eternal Father and the Divine Spirit is also received; here are all the Vertues, Charity, Hope, Purity, Patience, and Humility: because Christ our Lord begets all Vertue in the Soul, by means of this heavenly Food: and what a Heart must the Ministers have to forbid the Soul so great a Happiness.

If one only degree of Grace is a gift of inestimable Value and so precious, that 'tis not to be bought for a thousand Worlds being a particle of God himself, and a formal participation of the Divine Nature, which makes us his Children and Friends, Heirs of Heaven, and the Habitation of the most Holy Trinity: and if never so little Grace be worth more than all the Vertues, Alms, and Penances, and the removing Mountains (as St. *Paul* says) and giving all away to the Poor, is a meer Nothing without Grace: How then can it be well to deprive the Faithful of the increase of Grace, which he might find only in one Communion? How can the Minister deprive him of that and of many others that follow it, without giving 'em other things equivalent to those they lose?

What can be of equal value with habitual Grace, which a faithful Man might receive? neither can the Humility which he may exercise, nor the Reverence, nor the Mortification, upon the account of which he leaves off the Communion, be worth so much; nor are they equivalent to that Grace only, which he loses, and which he might have had by receiving that Communion.

And now lets make up this Account. If Restitution ought to be (as all the Doctors say) conformable to the Good, which was taken from one's Neighbour, what can he restore, which deprives a faithful Man of God himself?

Would it not be great want of Charity to take from a Man a Mount of Gold, only to gather up a little Grain? Only for one Grain of Mortification, (if yet there is any in it) the Ministers do deprive a Christian of a whole Mount of Blessings, which are heaped up together in the Communion: If there were no other way to mortifie and try the Soul, but this, it ought not to be used; because by this Mortification they deprive him of a greater good: but there are infinite ways of proving and mortifying the Soul besides, without doing it so great a Spiritual Prejudice.

The Blessings of this Sacrament don't end here; because, besides, the increase of Grace, it sustains and gives new strength to the Soul, to resist Temptations; it satisfies the desires, takes away the hunger of temporal things, unites with Christ and his Members, who are the Just and Righteous, breaks the power of Satan, gives strength to suffer Martyrdom, pardons the Venial Sins, to which he that Communicates doth not stand affected; and keeps from Mortal Sins, by vertue of the aid which it doth contribute.

The Body of Christ (says St. Bernard, *an Serm. Dom.*) is Medicine to the Sick, Provision for the Pilgrim, fresh Strength to the Weary, it delights the Strong, it heals the wounded, it preserves the Health of Soul and Body. And whoever is a worthy Communicant, is made more strong to receive Contempt, more patient to suffer Reproof, more fit to indure Troubles, more ready for Obedience, and to return the Lord Thanks.

St. Leo Pope (*de præc. ser. 14. de pass. Domini*) says, that when a man is Communicated, Christ comes to honour him with his Presence, to anoint him with his Grace, to cure him with his Mercy, to heal him with his Blood, to raise him by his Death, to illuminate him with his Light, to inflame him with his Love, to comfort him with his infinite Sweetness, to be united and espoused with his Soul, to make him partaker of his Divine Spirit, and of all the Blessings which he purchas'd us by his Cross.

Dost thou seek (says St. Bonaventure, *de præc.*) where God is? thou must expect to find him in this Divine Sacrament, which being worthily received, does pardon Sins, mittigate Passions, gives light to the Understanding, satiates the Soul, revives Faith, encourages Hope, inkindles Charity, increases Devotion, fills with Grace, and is the rich Pledge of Glory.

This Sacrament (says St. Thomas Opusc, *58. de Sacr. cap. 21, 22, 23*) drives away evil Spirits, defends us from Concupiscence, washes off the Stains of the Heart, appeases Gods Anger, illuminates the Understanding, to know him inflames the Will, to love him, delights the memory with Sweetness, confirms the whole man in Goodness, frees him from Punishment Everlasting, multiplies the merits of good Life, and brings him to his Eternal Country. The Body of the Lord (as he pursues it, *cap.* 24.) produces Three principal Effects. First, it destroys Sin. Secondly, it increases Spiritual Blessings. Thirdly, it comforts men's Souls; and in Chap. 25 he says, it satiates the Spirit to follow what is good; it comforts and strengthens the Soul, to shun what is evil, it preserves the Life always to praise the Lord. As it is a Sacrifice, it remits the Sins of those who are a live, and lightens the punishment of those who are in Purgatory, and augments the accidental Glory of those who are in Heaven. Lastly, the Body of Christ is called the Sacrament of Charity; because it makes us partakers of the Spirit Divine, of the sweet Abode of Christ himself, and the rich Transformation of God.

'Twould be an endless thing to relate the Blessings, which, according to the saying of Saints, they do receive from this Sacrament, who come to partake of it without Mortal Sin: and of all these doth the Minister deprive a Christian, when he only forbids him one Communion.

But more than this, depriving 'em of the Communion, he deprieves all the Saints of Heaven, all the Angels, the most holy Virgin, and Christ himself of that accidental glory which accrues to them by every Communion received in grace. If the Saints in Heaven have a special accidental glory, by every good work, though never so small, that is done here below, as many pious Authors are of opinion, with how much more reason will they have it by a work so sublime as the Communion is, wherein there is included an immensity of all the wonderful works of God? *Memoriam fecit mirabilium suorum,* Psal. 110.

And if from one only Communion there are so many blessings, as are specified before, to be obtained, what will there be of the sacrifice of the Mass, the gravest, the highest work that is in Heaven or Earth? And shall there then be, Ministers, who under pretence of Penance, Mortification, or the old way, must hinder Priests so great, so holy, and so fruitful a sacrifice?

Saint Jerom said, (*in Missis defunct. Pavi. c. 14.*) that at the least the Soul suffers not in Purgatory, whilst Mass is said for it ['twas well the Author did not point to us where this blind passage is, in *Saint Jeromes Works.*] *Saint Austin* assures us, (*Ballester in the Book of the Crucifix of S. Saviour, f. 207.*) that the Divine Sacrifice is never Celebrated, but one of these two things follow upon it, either the Conversion of a sinner, or the leting loose of some Soul out of Purgatory, [this is a much Saint *Austins* saying, as t'other is Saint *Jeromes.*] William Altisiodorensis was not contented with one Soul; but affirmed, that by every Mass there were the Lord knows how many Souls that got away from thence. Severius in *St. Martin's Life* gives an account that he set as many souls at liberty with his Masses, as persons assisted at the hearing of 'em.

Venerable Bede says, that the Priest, who, being not lawfully hindred, doth neglect to say Mass, deprives the most holy Trinity of glory and praise, the Angels of joy, Sinners of pardon, the Righteous of grace and help, the souls in Purgatory of cooling and refreshment, the Church of the heavenly benefit of Jesus Christ our Lord, and the Priest himself of Medicine and help.

If every Mass therefore has all this of its own, what Minister under the colour of zeal shall be so bold as to hinder and defraud the Trinity, the Angels, the Virgin, the Church, the Righteous, Sinners, the Souls in Purgatory, and the Priests themselves that desire to celebrate, so much glory and so much good? without doubt though this be done with zeal, yet 'tis want of consideration, and it will be well, to premeditate and consider it better, before any goes about to hinder it.

THE END.

Made in the USA
Columbia, SC
03 January 2019